The
Curriculum Vitae
Handbook

For

Judy Hendershot,
again

The
Curriculum Vitae
Handbook

How to Present and Promote
Your Academic Career

Second Edition

Rebecca Anthony & Gerald Roe

Rudi Publishing • San Francisco

Rudi Publishing, 12 Geary St., Suite 508, San Francisco CA 94108

ISBN 0-945213-26-3

First Edition 1994

PRINTED IN THE UNITED STATES OF AMERICA

Library of Congress Cataloging-in-Publication Data

Anthony, Rebecca
        The curriculum vitae handbook : how to present and promote your academic
    career / Rebecca Anthony & Gerald Roe. —2nd ed.
                p. cm.
        Includes index.
        ISBN 0-945213-26-3
        1. College teachers—Employment—United States. 2. Résumés
    (Employment)—United States.   3. College teaching—Vocational guidance—
    United States.   I. Roe, Gerald.   II. Title.
    LB2331.72.A58   1998
    378.1'2'02373—dc21   98-7277
                                                                  CIP

Contents

Acknowledgments

We would like to thank Douglas J. Swenson, Karen Southard, Deanna Hurst, Brian Lewis, James Huberty, and J. Joe Bishop who generously shared ideas and materials for this edition. We are indebted to Bruce Drummond for technical advice and assistance. In addition, of course, our gratitude is extended to the thousands of people who, over many years, have shared with us the summaries of their professsional lives.

Preface

The first edition of this book proposed a fresh look at how a CV is constructed and how it is used. Although a CV is indispensable at any stage of an academic career, most people first discover a need for a CV when they are beginning a professional job search. The current edition continues the emphasis on the development and use of a CV for employment purposes, with additional attention to the multiple uses of the CV in career development.

Samples of effective CVs have been created to illustrate the different stages of an academic career and the different applications which require a version of a CV. The samples are intended to serve as useful models whether you are designing your first CV in order to enter the academic job market or reconstructing and redirecting an earlier version to reflect new interests or to present your accomplishments and achievements to a new audience.

Rebecca Anthony
Gerald Roe
April, 1998

Demystifying the CV

Academics value precise language. In order to say exactly what they mean, academics often ascribe specific meaning to words that the general public uses less exactly. Similarly, the language of the academy draws upon a vocabulary larger, richer, and more complex than most of us use in ordinary conversation; professors may speak of paradigms and parameters to one audience, of models and limits to another.

The name we give to a particular thing is only a label. As Juliet says, "that which we call a rose by any other name would smell as sweet." But the distinctive feature of the rose, its particular aromatic character, would delight our senses and linger in our memories whether we refer to the rose by some less mellifluous name or lump it into the general category of "flower."

Without precise definitions or universally acknowledged distinctions, the terms *résumé* and *CV*, the abbreviation of *curriculum vitae*, and *vita* have been subject to personal opinions, biases, and esoteric interpretations. The terms are not synonymous, but attempts to distinguish between them have never been completely successful. Myths and misconceptions about the nature and use of these respective documents have been handed down from one generation of academics to another, sometimes assuming a false sanctity along with the mantle of tradition. Some have contended that definition is a matter of length: a résumé is short, ideally consisting of a single sheet; a CV is a more comprehensive document consisting of several pages. This simplistic distinction is arbitrary and inaccurate; content, not length, should be of paramount consideration.

Unfortunately, dictionaries are no help. *Webster's New Twentieth Century Dictionary* defines vita as "the summary of one's personal history and professional qualifications, as that submitted by a job applicant; résumé." A résumé is defined as: "a summing up, a summary."

It is time to establish a clear and useful definition of these terms.

Résumé. A résumé is a document that summarizes qualifications, education, experience, skills, and other items related to the writer's objective. Legitimate entries could include non-academic pursuits, civic or community activities, even leisure interests.

CV. A CV is a special type of résumé traditionally used within the academic community. Earned degrees, teaching and research experience, publications, presentations, and related activities are featured.

In short, a CV is an academic version of a résumé. This simple statement eliminates unnecessary confusion and directs attention to the real differences between the terms.

Your CV Is a Lifelong Companion

For an academic, a CV is a multi-purpose and perpetually unfinished document, a cumulative record of professional achievements from graduate student to professor emeritus. It is not, however, a permanent record, nor is it static; your CV is flexible, adaptable, capable of reflecting changes in your responsibilities, activities, and accomplishments, and shifting emphases to suit your purpose.

Your CV is an integral part of your professional image. The format, the style, even much of the content of your original CV must be evaluated in light of subsequent experiences, your present position, and career objectives.

Develop the habit of revising your CV regularly. A publication, a presentation, a new committee assignment—any professional development—could necessitate an update. A continuously maintained rough draft can eliminate the pressure of hastily reconstructing your professional history to meet a deadline.

However minor the revision, a new copy must be printed before you can submit it to a search committee, a review board, a publisher, even to the person who will introduce you as a guest lecturer. It is never a good practice to update a CV with handwritten changes or additions.

Maintaining an effective CV requires more than periodic updating. As your career progresses and your CV changes, just keeping it current is not sufficient to project your strongest assets. Instead of merely adding entries to your existing CV, consider a thorough revision. Create new categories to reflect your interests, responsibilities, and achievements. Delete items no longer relevant to your objective, and reorganize the sections to emphasize current strengths.

Whether you are contemplating yet another revision or attempting your very first CV, solicit comments and suggestions from advisors, mentors, and colleagues. A reader's perspective can detect gaps, errors, or inconsistencies. You might receive helpful suggestions for items you had not thought of including, or valuable advice about organizing your presentation.

Expect widely divergent opinions about what is necessary and desirable in a CV. Some of the advice you receive could be conflicting or contradictory. Consider all suggestions carefully, and incorporate only those that make sense to you. Balance the opinions of well-meaning associates against your own convictions. Your understanding of the purpose and use of a CV will enable you to discriminate among suggestions that merely reflect outmoded traditions or individual biases, and those that can enhance the quality and increase the effect of your CV.

Your CV is a lifelong companion. You will never write a final version.

Promoting Yourself in the Academic Marketplace

The hiring process for academics is significantly different from the typical practices of business or industry. The terminology, the protocol, the time span, the diverse complexities of a committee-based screening and selection process, and the sheer bulk of the required papers and documents characterize and distinguish academic employment practices. In most cases, competition for academic positions is intense and prolonged.

Outside the academic world, applications for most jobs are routinely received and processed by a human resources office or a personnel department. Even for entry-level positions, however, academic professionals are usually selected by a committee of individuals assembled solely for the purpose of identifying a pool of applicants, interviewing selected candidates, and recommending one of the finalists for a particular position.

Because members of the selection committee must continue their own teaching, advising, and research activities while writing the job description for the available position, circulating the vacancy announcement, collecting applications, accepting nominations, narrowing the field to a select few, and scheduling and conducting interviews, the process can take several months.

Through your graduate studies you have acquired sophistication and assurance within your academic discipline. Your thorough preparation should make you confident about beginning your career, but far more than subject-area expertise is involved in obtaining a position. Even the brightest and most promising graduate students sometimes feel unsure and uneasy about the prospect of securing suitable employment.

In order to be selected for the position you desire, you must appreciate academic hiring practices and you must promote your skills and abilities to potential employers. Many academics are uncomfortable with the idea of self-promotion. The thought of marketing oneself frequently conjures up distasteful images of hard-sell tactics. Nevertheless, entering the academic marketplace demands that you develop a persuasive means of communicating your qualifications. For that purpose, the most effective tool is a CV.

Using Your CV

Although it has many uses, a CV is the cornerstone of a successful job search. Your CV introduces you, outlines your background, interests, and experiences, and establishes your professional image.

Creating a favorable impression is important at every stage of the employment process, but never more so than at first contact. When you have the opportunity to interview with a potential employer, you pay special attention to your clothing, your grooming, your manner, even your tone of voice. The first person you meet might simply direct you to someone else, either an individual or a group, who will make ultimate decisions about your candidacy for the position.

Just as in a typical interview, you would meet several different people, your CV must pass through the hands of many individuals, each with a set of responsibilities and attitudes, and with varying degrees of interest in your career. Your CV might first be handled by someone whose only concern is to refer it to the appropriate desk. There it is screened and relayed to the next stage, eventually reaching a point that will determine its fate.

As your representative, your CV must convey a consistent professional image whether it is merely glanced at, quickly scanned, read with some attention, or closely scrutinized.

During the Job Search

A CV is important at each of the following stages of your job search:

Job Inquiries. If you are interested in working at a particular institution, or if you need to locate in a specific geographic area, it is appropriate to forward a copy of your CV along with a letter inquiring about possible employment opportunities.

Advertised Jobs. Positions are advertised in academic and professional journals, newsletters, college placement bulletins, and by postings on departmental bulletin boards. In response to an announced vacancy, always send a copy of your CV with an appropriate cover letter.

Interviews. As a part of the screening process, each member of the search committee should have had the opportunity to review your CV; however, committee members may not have a copy available for reference. Take several copies with you to any interview. Offer copies of your CV as needed. Providing a copy to each member of the committee may facilitate interview questions and will assure you that each person is aware of your qualifications and experiences. In addition, your CV can serve as a helpful reminder after the interview.

Application Forms. Most colleges and universities do not require applicants to complete a standardized application form. Some institutions, especially community colleges and vocational schools, use an application form as a uniform method of collecting information from each applicant. These forms vary in length from a single sheet to complex multi-page packets. Read all application materials carefully before you begin to complete them. Application blanks can be frustrating; applicants frequently complain about being instructed to type their responses on forms that neither fit into a typewriter nor allow sufficient space. Certainly, applications are time-consuming, but your CV is not a substitute for a completed form. Use it as a handy reference for dates of employment and education, or other requested information. You can and should provide a copy of your CV with the completed application form.

Never simply write "See CV" on the employer's application form; this is a dangerous shortcut because your application could be considered incomplete.

References. Even before you begin to apply for positions, identifying people who can recommend you to potential employers is a critical step. A copy of your CV will enable your recommenders to provide accurate information and to focus their comments appropriately. This is particularly important for people with whom you have not been in continued or recent contact—but even current teachers, colleagues, or supervisors can benefit from having your CV at their fingertips. Your CV can enable them to write effective letters or to respond to telephone inquiries with ease and without hesitation.

Unforgettable as you may be, dates and details are not always correctly recalled. Your CV helps your recommenders help you.

Beyond the Job Search

In addition to using your CV for employment purposes, you will find many other occasions to submit a comprehensive or condensed version of this versatile document. Develop the habit of updating your CV frequently. As your career develops, you will use your CV in the following situations or activities:

Merit/Tenure Reviews. Your department, college, or university may have specific guidelines for materials to be submitted for merit or tenure considerations. A CV submitted for these purposes needs to provide thorough documentation of all teaching responsibilities, publications, presentations, research activities, and academic service.

Publishing. When you submit a manuscript proposal to an academic journal or press, your CV can efficiently establish your credibility by summarizing your academic preparation and previous professional publications.

Grant Applications. Any request for internal or external support for research or project development is routinely accompanied by a CV for each principal investigator or project manager and for key personnel. Relevant emphases include previous funding, a record of activity in appropriate fields, and evidence of research and technical competencies.

Speaking Engagements. A condensed one- to two-page version of your CV listing degrees, employment, a summary of publications with titles of recent or most significant books or articles, and other honors or distinctions can provide information useful for publicity or appropriate introductions.

Consulting. When you offer your services as a consultant, your CV provides information about your areas of expertise directly relevant to the needs of the institution or organization. The exact nature of the consulting opportunity should indicate the need for a comprehensive or a condensed CV.

Leadership Roles, Awards, or Special Recognitions. Nominating committees frequently request background information from candidates for elected office. Selection committees also review contributions and service in evaluating individuals for honors or prizes. In either case, a CV presents a record of leadership experience and scholarly, creative, or other appropriate professional activities.

Sabbatical or Fellowship Opportunities. As a supplement to any required application materials, submit your CV to document scholarly achievements and requisite competencies. Your CV can offer details not specifically requested as well as reinforcing information already provided.

Prepare Your Own CV

You are probably aware that the general public does not have a clear or accurate understanding of academic careers. The responsibilities, the concerns, and even the language of the academic world can be confusing and intimidating to people outside the profession.

Few commercial résumé writers are equipped to deal with the special needs of an academic CV. Save your money and your time—you are the person best able to put your CV together.

Hire a word processing expert or a skilled typist to deal with the mechanics of producing a final copy if your skills are inadequate or if you're pressed for time. This modest expense will allow you to concentrate on more important activities related to your job search. Relinquishing control is a mistake. Don't expect a commercial résumé writer to do your work for you.

Allowing another person to prepare your CV is risky; there is a very real danger that the result will be an impersonal document that fails to reflect you as an academic or even as an individual. It may look more like a business résumé than an academic CV. The content of your CV creates a critical first impression that contributes to your complete professional profile.

11

The finished product—the CV you submit to a potential employer—should not be prepared by anyone else. Your careful consideration of the content and format makes it possible to focus on your special attributes and abilities.

CV Format

Contemporary hiring practices, along with a constantly fluctuating job market and dramatic advances in communications technology, make it necessary for today's job seeker to challenge conventional thinking about CV preparation and to abandon outmoded traditions.

The Model CV

The notion of one correct and proper format for every CV is a persistent myth. This hypothetical standard is unwittingly fostered and perpetuated through samples prepared by many professional associations. With good intentions of providing a service, particularly to junior members, the association designs and distributes a single example that too often becomes the prescriptive model for the discipline. Even if it is not particularly well suited to their individual needs, job seekers are reluctant to depart from what they perceive to be the officially sanctioned format.

Faculty advisors and other mentors, too, can help to perpetuate the myth of the standard or correct format for a CV. They are likely to have created their own CVs in the likeness of an earlier prototype. It is probable that little modification or alteration was attempted. Or required. It is worth remembering that the majority of today's senior faculty entered a very different sort of job market.

The truth is, no single format will meet the needs of all job seekers. The sample CVs in this book illustrate formats that are both professional in appearance and flexible enough to accommodate varying amounts of material.

Forcing your material to fit into a prescribed form is unnecessarily restrictive. Give yourself the freedom to adapt any model to your unique situation.

Design your CV to emphasize your strengths and your achievements.

CV Length

The notion that a résumé is shorter than a CV is a common misconception. A CV is distinguished from a résumé not by its length but by its content.

The relevance of the information presented is more significant than the total number of pages filled. The CV prepared by a Ph.D. is not necessarily longer or more detailed than the one submitted by someone with a master's degree. The length of your CV is not dependent upon academic degrees you have earned, the professorial rank you have attained or the number of years spanned by your career. Any academic should maintain a complete account of all professional achievements, publications, presentations, recognitions, and collegial activities. Pages can add up quickly. The complete record is typically required for internal review for tenure, promotion, or merit considerations. For any use outside the department, college, or university, the complete CV would serve as source material for a condensed version appropriately focused.

It's not unusual for productive academics to accumulate enough material to fill many pages. At first glance, compared to your own brief CV, your advisor or mentor's CV may resemble a hefty manuscript. Don't be intimidated by this sheaf of material and don't think yours has to imitate it. At the beginning of your career, you are not measured against experienced professionals. Your competition is with your peers.

Nor should your CV be subject to the restrictions of the business world, which traditionally claims to prefer a one-page résumé.

Your CV can not conform to arbitrary standards established for a different work environment and culture. Except for the most obvious parallels, the process of screening and selection is not comparable. For an academic to follow the dictates of the business community is foolishly short-sighted.

CV Content

There are very few rules about the content of a CV, and there are many different activities or experiences that can appropriately be included. However, every CV must present three essential elements:

- Name and address
- Education
- Relevant experience

These are indispensable. You must tell prospective employers who you are and how you can be reached. You must tell them what degrees you hold or are in the process of completing. And you must describe relevant experiences or skills.

Identification

Your name, address, and telephone number should be clearly stated. Home, office, and electronic mail addresses may be listed, along with telephone and fax numbers (with area codes).

To avoid confusion, the name you use on your CV should be consistent with other supporting documents such as transcripts, letters of recommendation, and licenses. Discrepancies could result in your application being considered incomplete.

To maintain a professional identity, you can elect to use either your birth name or an adopted name for all but social purposes. You have the legal right to use any name you choose, so long as there is no attempt to conceal your true identity or to defraud.

If you change your surname but your previous name is retained on transcripts or other official documents, be sure the person or office receiving your application materials is aware of both names.

Nicknames or variations of your first name should be avoided. After you have been hired, you will have the opportunity to let your colleagues know your preferred name. In any job search, it is your responsibility to use consistent names or to make the potential employer aware of any possible discrepancies.

Education

Your CV should include information about graduate and undergraduate degrees including:
- academic discipline
- names and locations of degree-granting institutions
- dates degrees conferred

Unlike a transcript, your CV is not an official document. You have the option to include dates of attendance, registration for specific courses, and grade point averages. It is your decision to list or to exclude attendance at institutions other than those granting your degrees.

In some cases, it is to your advantage to list attendance at other institutions even if a degree was not earned. Reasons to provide this information could include specialized study, geographic locations, or type of institution.

For example, a musician might emphasize professional courses or private study with a master teacher; a graduate of a large state university might list attendance at a small private college; anyone could choose to include foreign study.

Relevant Experience

List teaching, research, and related experience including graduate assistantships, internships or postdoctoral fellowships. If the job title is insufficient to convey the extent or the value of your experience, brief descriptions of responsibilities or duties are usually to your advantage.

This is one place where you can legitimately indulge in name-dropping. Capitalize on the reputation of a mentor who enjoys national or international recognition. Only your qualifications will get you a job; your mentor's professional status can get you noticed.

Caution: Accuracy about academic degrees and experiences is critical. Even the slightest discrepancy can be damaging.

Even if all requirements have been met, do not state that you hold a degree until it has been officially conferred. Include an annotation explaining that all requirements are completed and the degree will be conferred on a particular date.

The discovery of inaccuracies, untruths, or misrepresentations will usually preclude further consideration of your candidacy. Once hired, the discovery that you have provided false information can be cause for termination.

Employers and the courts take fraud very seriously. Protect yourself and your career by telling the truth.

CV Categories

An effective CV conveys much more than the three essentials. Options are almost unlimited because they reflect the unique background, experiences, interests, and preferences of the writer.

The words and phrases in your CV can help to establish a tone which should be consistent with your writing style and can even indicate something of your personality.

Choose category headings that emphasize your strengths and achievements and that are most appropriate to your particular discipline or field of interest.

The following list includes a variety of terms which can help you to identify and arrange items of importance and interest to employers.

Suggested CV Categories

Education

Educational Background

Educational Overview

Formal Education

Professional Studies

Academic Background

Academic Preparation

Academic Training

Degrees

Principal Teachers

Dissertation

Dissertation Title

Dissertation Topic

Comprehensive Areas

Master's project

Thesis

Professional Competencies

Course Highlights

Educational Highlights

Proficiencies

Areas of Knowledge

Areas of Expertise

Areas of Experience

Areas of Concentration in Graduate
    Study

Graduate Fieldwork

Graduate Practica

Specialized Training

Internships

Teaching/Research Assistantships

Teaching Interests

Academic Interests

Research Interests

Educational Interests

Postdoctoral Experience

Professional Interests

Professional Experience

Professional Overview

Professional Background

Academic Appointments

Current Academic Appointments

Teaching Experience

Teaching Overview

Experience Summary

Professional Summary

Experience Highlights

Related Professional Experience

Research Appointments

Research Experience

Academic Accomplishments

Professional Achievements

Suggested CV Categories

Career Achievements

Career Highlights

Background

Research Overview

Administrative Experience

Consulting Experience

Consultantships

Continuing Education Experience

Related Experiences

Academic Service

Advising

Professional Service

Professional Development

University Involvement

Service

Outreach

Faculty Leadership

Major Committees

Committee Leadership

Departmental Leadership

Professional Association Advisory
Boards

Major University Assignments

Advisory Committees

National Boards

Conferences Attended

Conference Participation

Conference Presentation

Conference Leadership

Workshop Presentations

Convention Addresses

Invited Addresses

Invited Lectures

Lectures and Colloquia

Scholarly Presentations

Programs and Workshops

Professional Activities

Presentations and Publications

Abstracts

Publications

Scholarly Publications

Scholarly Works

Bibliography

Books

Chapters

Editorial Boards

Professional Papers

Technical Papers

Refereed Journal Articles

Editorial Appointments

Articles/Monographs

Reviews

Book Reviews

Multimedia Materials

Suggested CV Categories

Selected Presentations	Professional Memberships
Research Awards	Memberships in Scholarly Societies
Research Grants	Professional Organizations
Funded Projects	Honorary Societies
Grants and Contracts	Professional Societies
Patents	Professional Certification
Exhibits/Exhibitions	Certification
Arrangements/Scores	Licensure
Performances	Endorsements
Recitals	Special Training
Scholarships	Foreign Study
Fellowships	Study Abroad
Academic Awards	Travel Abroad
Honors	International Projects
Distinctions	Languages
College Distinctions	Language Competencies
Activities and Distinctions	
Honors and Awards	Dossier
Professional Recognition	Credentials
Prizes	Placement File
College Activities	Portfolio
Awards	Recommendations
Affiliations	References
Memberships	

Style and Substance

In many categories, simply listing information may not adequately convey your achievements or contributions. Three categories, for example, call for expansion or amplification. Give careful consideration to the details of your major accomplishments.

Publications. List all professional publications using the bibliographic style prescribed for your discipline. The guidelines you have used for preparing scholarly papers will serve for this purpose. If you have any questions, consult appropriate manuals. For example, *The Chicago Manual of Style, The MLA Style Manual* or the *Publication Manual of the American Psychological Association* provide examples for proper listing of books, periodicals, technical and research reports, theses, unpublished manuscripts, reviews, etc. Works accepted for publication should be included; materials submitted for consideration are optional.

Grants. A demonstrated knowledge of grant writing is an asset; any successful experience in securing funding from internal sources or outside agencies should be documented. Identify the project, the funding agency, and dollar amount if appropriate. You may also list participation in grant preparation even if you were not the principal investigator or the recipient of funding.

Performances/Exhibitions. Performers and visual artists must include information about recitals, roles, exhibits, shows, and recognitions. The categories can be divided into several sections, if necessary, to highlight accomplishments. A printmaker, for example, could divide exhibitions into juried shows, solo shows, and group shows, and include categories to document awards, works in public or private collections, and gallery affiliations.

Irrelevant Information

Federal and state guidelines prohibit employers from basing hiring decisions on such characteristics as the applicant's age, sex, race, religion, disability, and national origin.

Employers are allowed to collect information about these characteristics on a special form, usually distributed by and returned to the institution's Office of Affirmative Action. Such forms are not intended to be a part of the application file, but are used to document characteristics of the pool of applicants, those interviewed, and the individual hired. Collecting this information enables the employer to demonstrate compliance with federal legislation and state employment guidelines.

Legal restrictions do not prohibit you from offering personal information—you are free to mention any of these characteristics or any other vital statistic you choose to present (height, weight, marital status, dependents). But to do so is unnecessary, unsophisticated, and usually unwise.

Your CV is not your autobiography. Keep the focus on your job-related abilities and potential. Inappropriate information can divert attention from the more important elements of your CV detailing your professional qualifications and achievements.

Tell employers what they need to know, not necessarily everything they might want to know. Biases exist. There is no need to trigger them prematurely. Advertising autobiographical details in your CV may close more doors than it will open.

Personal Data.

No photograph

No race, religion, ethnicity

No age, date, or place of birth

No physical characteristics (gender, height, weight, eye color)

No family information (marital status, name and occupation of spouse, names and ages of children)

Action Words = Interest

The words and phrases you select to describe your experiences and qualifications contribute to your professional image. Clear, direct communication should be your primary goal.

Your CV is not the place for long, eloquent paragraphs or even for compound sentences. Use short sentences or phrases. Sentence fragments are perfectly acceptable; fragments allow you to omit the overused personal pronoun.

Make it easy for the reader to obtain information quickly. "Organized a seminar for student teachers," effectively and economically conveys the same concept as "I was responsible for the organization of a seminar for student teachers."

The following list of action words will help your CV—and you—appear more dynamic, more interesting, and more appealing.

Action Words		
abstracted	awarded	defined
accomplished	budgeted	delivered
achieved	catalogued	demonstrated
acquired	chaired	derived
acted	coauthored	described
adapted	collaborated	designed
addressed	collected	determined
adjudicated	communicated	developed
advised	compiled	diagnosed
analyzed	completed	directed
approved	composed	discovered
articulated	computed	drafted
arranged	conducted	earned
assessed	consulted	edited
assimilated	contracted	elected
assisted	coordinated	elicited
authored	counseled	encouraged
automated	created	established

Action Words

evaluated	measured	represented
examined	monitored	researched
exhibited	motivated	reviewed
expanded	negotiated	revised
facilitated	nominated	scheduled
formulated	observed	screened
founded	operated	selected
generated	organized	served
guided	originated	solved
identified	participated	sponsored
illustrated	performed	standardized
implemented	planned	streamlined
improved	predicted	strengthened
increased	prepared	structured
individualized	presented	studied
initiated	presided	supervised
installed	prioritized	synthesized
instructed	processed	taught
integrated	projected	tested
interpreted	promoted	trained
interviewed	produced	transformed
introduced	programmed	translated
invented	published	tutored
investigated	quantified	unified
judged	recommended	updated
lectured	recognized	verified
maintained	recruited	volunteered
managed	registered	wrote
mastered	reorganized	

First Draft

Get your story down on paper. Don't worry about the length, the arrangement, the appearance, or even about the importance of the information. At this point, your concern should simply be to list all possible items that could be included in your CV.

Editing comes later.

Once you have listed your experiences, activities, and educational background, you can begin to think about the effect each item will have on the reader. You may determine that some less relevant items should be deleted, and others expanded to provide more detail. A useful strategy for expansion is to annotate entries that demonstrate required or desirable skills. For example, the term *teaching assistant* covers a wide range of responsibilities. A teaching assistant may help to grade student work or lead discussion sections following a lecture by a member of the faculty. The same term may be applied to an instructor who is fully responsible for all aspects of the course. Briefly delineating the duties is the only way to ensure that the reader understands the extent of your responsibilities and the nature of your experience.

Arranging CV Categories

As you begin to think about the order or placement of items on your CV, consider the following:

- If you have recently completed or are about to complete a degree program, placing the education information first is to your advantage. This section tells the employer that you have the requisite academic qualifications and also accounts for your most recent activities.
- Categories dealing with teaching or research interests are most effective near the beginning of a CV because they influence the reader's perception of all subsequent information. Listing teaching or research interests allows you to indicate competencies that cannot be demonstrated by experience. These categories can be modified or even eliminated depending upon the emphasis desired.

Categories can be combined to make more efficient use of space or to enable you to include information that might appear out of place or insubstantial if listed in a separate category.

For example, you might include a single published paper with a series of conference presentations under the category of Professional Activities or Presentations and Publications rather than listing one item in a separate Publications category. You can include academic honors or distinctions in conjunction with the appropriate educational program or degree rather than taking valuable space to create another category heading with only one or two entries.

Rearranging categories of information allows you to create different versions of your CV for different purposes. If you are seeking a job, it is to your advantage to emphasize the aspects of your experience that you expect to be of greater interest to the school or department you seek to join.

Start with the information you consider vital. Build on your strengths, through several drafts, if necessary. Don't rush toward a final version. Give yourself time to think, to evaluate, to experiment, to revise. As with any serious writing, revision is essential to producing an effective and interesting CV.

CV Production

Once you get past the draft and revise stage, it is time to think about methods of producing a finished version. Personal computers make it relatively easy to move from the rough draft to a finished document that is attractive, professional in appearance and design, and inexpensive.

You don't have to be a dedicated hacker to make your CV look as if it had been professionally prepared. With any word processing system and a good printer, there are a myriad of fonts (type styles and sizes) literally at your fingertips and you have nearly unlimited possibilities for arranging your material and creating an effective page design. Clarity and emphasis can be achieved by underlining, boldface, italics, simple graphic techniques such as horizontal lines, frames, shading and symbols (• ○ ■ ◆).

Margins and spacing can be adjusted to accommodate your text and to enhance readability. Large amounts of material may require a long line with narrow margins; on the other hand, a short line with wide margins can fill out a page without resorting to obvious stretching or padding.

In either case, it is essential to allow sufficient white space to create an effective and visually pleasing document.

Your goal is to prepare a CV that can be read easily and quickly. Using several different fonts or graphics can divert attention from the content. One font is usually all you need. Emphasis can be achieved by adjusting the point size or employing other features such as bold print or italics. Be cautious about using large print throughout your CV. It is more difficult to scan and it may subtly suggest to the reader an attempt to inflate limited content.

Use the best printer you can. A clear, sharp image is mandatory.

Good quality bond paper is probably worth the small investment required. White or a neutral color is appropriate; do not spend much of your time attempting to select the exact shade of beige, light gray, or off white that will attract attention by its distinctive appearance. There is no evidence that any particular color or texture of paper is more effective than another. Furthermore, the original may not be circulated; it is much more likely to be photocopied for distribution to members of the search committee.

To assure that your CV retains its professional appearance even after being photocopied, your best choice is plain white paper. Agonize, if you must, over the content of your CV—not over the color or weight of your paper.

The Electronic CV

Innovations in electronic communication, combined with the proliferation of personal computers, have profoundly affected the process by which people are selected for employment. Even in academe, it is now possible to have your CV instantly transmitted electronically anywhere in the world or posted on the Internet for round-the-clock global accessibility.

Before you can submit your CV to an employer using electronic mail (e-mail), you will need to save your document as "text only" in an ASCII (American Standards Committee for Information Interchange) file. ASCII is capable of recognizing text, but formatting codes, graphics, some punctuation marks, special fonts, and highlighting features such as bold type, italics, centering, or underlining, are not compatible with current ASCII features.

Your electronic CV (whether printed or viewed on a computer screen)is likely to be quite different in appearance from your carefully designed paper version. With most e-mail systems, four or five lines at the top of the screen will be devoted to the sender's name and e-mail address, the recipient's e-mail address, and a subject line.

Only a limited portion of your CV will appear on the screen, so it is imperative that the first few lines tell the reader something about your immediate employment objectives. You may need to revise your CV if your traditional printed CV does not clearly identify your teaching or research interests. You might consider moving your address, phone numbers, etc., to the end of the document so that your name and your employment interests are clearly visible at the beginning of your CV.

To: Search Committee Chair
From: aj-borwn@umich.edu
Subject: Accounting Opening
Cc:
Bcc:
Attached:

AMANDA J. BROWN

TEACHING & RESEARCH INTERESTS
Cost accounting; corporate financial reporting
Regulation and financial analysis models; accounting information systems

EDUCATION
THE UNIVERSITY OF MICHIGAN, Ann Arbor, Michigan
Ph.D. Candidate in Accounting, May 2000
Dissertation Topic: Valuation and Reporting

The length of an electronic CV can be an issue. Even a single page of your CV will likely require the reader to scroll or page down once or twice to view the complete page. An electronic CV should be relatively short to maintain reader interest and, for the same reason, should avoid dense blocks of single-spaced text.

Electronic CV Headings. The ASCII format will not allow you to use conventional highlighting techniques such as bold, italics, or different fonts, so you will need to depend upon capital letters to provide limited emphasis. Capital letters are perhaps best used for category headings, since e-mail convention discourages the use of capital letters within the text.

To:	Search Committee Chair
From:	jsmithe@uga.edu
Subject:	CV-Instructional Design
Cc:	
Bcc:	
Attached:	

JAMIE SMITHE

DEGREES

Ph.D. INSTRUCTIONAL DESIGN & TECHNOLOGY
University of Georgia, Athens, Georgia, 1997-present

M.A. COMPUTER SCIENCE Iowa State University, Ames, Iowa, 1994-1996

B.A. HISTORY with honors, Grinnell College, Grinnell, Iowa, 1992

World Wide Web

The Internet and the World Wide Web make it possible to have your CV accessible to anyone, anywhere in the world, at any time. In addition, a CV created in Hypertext Markup Language (HTML) affords the opportunity to include images, sounds, video clips, and other features for a true multimedia presentation. Using available technology it is possible to create a home page that incorporates not only an electronic CV but a professional portfolio with links to samples of your scholarly or creative work, but avocations, hobbies, family information, and photographs of yourself should not appear.

The CV you put out on the World Wide Web should provide links only to your e-mail address and to sites containing material you have created (syllabi, statement of teaching interests or philosophy, scholarly papers, etc.). Links to other sites or to information not related to your professional goals and objectives can be distracting.

The address of your Web site or URL (Uniform Resource Locator) can appear with your address at the top of the paper version of your CV or at the bottom of your e-mail version.

Scanning Technology

In the business world, résumés submitted in response to an advertised position are frequently scanned electronically for key words of special significance to the responsibilities of the position. After sorting by keywords, a résumé can be entered into a database of potential employees.

Scanning has probably not yet been of much consequence in screening the CVs submitted by academics. As technology becomes cheaper and more sophisticated, however, the scanner will undoubtedly assume a more important role in the selection process. Academic departments could fairly easily determine key words for use in sorting through the CVs submitted for a particular position.

Textured or colored paper stock can pose problems for a scanner. Ordinary white paper, a standard font, no graphic features, and standard black print make it most likely that the CV can be scanned accurately.

Most scanners have no difficulty with standard fonts such as Courier or Helvetica but may not be able to read other fonts. At the present time, most scanners have some difficulty with graphics, including bullets, check marks, horizontal or vertical lines, text boxes, etc. Scanning software, however, like most computer programs, is constantly being refined.

The traditional CV on good quality paper is still very much a part of the screening and selection process for positions in academe. Advances in technology will undoubtedly change the method of submitting information, but hiring in the academic world is very far from becoming a "paperless" process.

CV Samples

The following samples illustrate various stages of academic careers, depicting students pursuing advanced degrees, recent graduates, and experienced professionals. The samples demonstrate logical arrangements of categories and concise presentation of content using appropriate terminology and action words and phrases. Although the samples have been limited to one or two pages, the models are not intended to suggest a maximum length.

Review several CVs before you begin to draft your own version. Look beyond those samples that most closely correspond to your academic discipline or level of experience. You can combine features of two or more different samples to emphasize your particular qualifications and to accentuate your strengths.

The samples in this section offer suggestions for formatting; no special relationship between format and discipline should be inferred.

Notice how strategic features identified for each CV contribute to its total effect. The special features are not necessarily related to the academic discipline but reflect the particular strengths of the writer or the specific requirements or responsibilities of a position held or desired.

Literature CV

Strategic Features

- Educational information is presented first to emphasize plans to complete the terminal degree

- Dissertation topic is identified as "projected," indicating probable areas of research

- Short annotations describe teaching and service responsibilities

∼

Take a careful look at this sample if

- your degree is in progress
- you have substantial pre-doctoral teaching experience

SAMUEL BUTLER
16 University Avenue, Any City, State 12345
(101) 555-0101
sbutler3@pennstate.edu

EDUCATION

Ph.D. **Comparative Literature**, 1999–present
The Pennsylvania State University, University Park, Pennsylvania
Projected Dissertation: *Three Writers In Transition: A Study in the Poetics of Influence in the Literature of Eduardo Pinero (Brazil), Mercedes Oliva (North America) and Alicia Javier (Argentina)*. Dissertation Advisor: Margarida Swey

M.A. **Comparative Literature**, 1996–1998
The Pennsylvania State University, University Park, Pennsylvania

B.A. **English & Spanish**, *magna cum laude*, 1990–1994
University of Oklahoma, Norman, Oklahoma

AWARDS

State of Oklahoma Scholar, 4 years
Dean's List and President's List
Murray International Scholarship

Rhodes Scholar finalist
Excellence in Teaching Award, 2000
University Award for Outstanding
Conference Paper, 1999

TEACHING EXPERIENCE

Department of English, 2000–present
Instructor, Saturday & Evening Division, The Pennsylvania State University
Taught two sections of Narrative Literature, one of the courses fulfilling the general education requirement for undergraduates.Classes included traditional and non-traditional students.

Department of English, 1999–present
Teaching Assistant, The Pennsylvania State University
Courses taught (total of 12 sections):
- *Narrative Literature*
- *Interpretation of Literature*
- *American Lives*
- *Lyric Poetry*

Department of Spanish, 1997–1999
Teaching Assistant, The Pennsylvania State University
Courses taught (total of 6 sections):
- *Elementary Spanish*
- *Spanish II*

DEPARTMENTAL/CAMPUS INVOLVEMENT

Co-chair, Course Review Committee for the course, American Lives.
Recommendations accepted by the General Education Program, 1999

Student member, Search Committee for the Vice President—Academic Affairs.
Reviewed application materials; participated in screening and selection process, 1998

Member, University Lecture Series Committee.
Responsible for reviewing credentials of proposed lecturers, for securing bids and booking contracts for campus lecturers, 1998-2000

PROFESSIONAL AFFILIATIONS

Modern Language Association
Society for Spanish & Portuguese Historical Studies

TRAVEL & LANGUAGES

Extensive travel in Europe, Asia, Central & South America:
- 2 years' residence with family in Faro, Brazil
- 1 year exchange program residence with family in Tuticorin, India

Languages: Spanish, Portuguese, French

RELATED EXPERIENCE

Peace Corps Volunteer, Belmopan, Belize, 1994-1996.
Duties included teaching English as a second language in village community centers. Taught all ages, from pre-school to retirement.

Tutor, Philadelphia Hispanic Center, summers, 1992-1995.
Taught English to non-English speaking immigrants in the evening program. Worked with adults and children in small group settings and one-on-one.

DOSSIER

Career Development & Placement Services, Any City, State 12345
(101) 555-1000 FAX: (101) 555-2000

Education CV
Strategic Features

- Academic Preparation clearly identifies degrees earned and in progress, and gives details about the anticipated dissertation and comprehensive areas

- Annotations of experiences use strong action phrases and specific details to capture the reader's interest

- Significant professional and leadership roles are accentuated by creating subheads within the category to direct attention to various areas of professional service

~

Take a careful look at this sample if

- you have several related experiences and research interests

- you require ample space to provide detailed annotations and listing of specific material

ALEXIA SAMPRAS

121 Academic Hall   Any City, State 12345
(101) 555-1111   a-sampras@usb.edu

ACADEMIC BACKGROUND:

Ph.D. Curriculum and Instruction Emphasis: Developmental Reading
University of Santa Barbara, Santa Barbara, California.
Anticipated May 2000
Dissertation title: *Developmentally Appropriate Learning Styles for the Student with Second Language Acquisition.* K. T. Russ, Ph.D. Adviser
Comprehensive areas: Elementary Education, Developmental Reading, English as a Second Language

M.A. Elementary Education - Bilingual Emphasis, 1995
Lewis and Clark University, Portland Oregon
Thesis: *Early Reading Patterns of Immigrant Children*, B.E. Fine, Ph.D. Adviser

B.A. Spanish and Elementary Education, 1990
University of Hawaii at Manoa   *cum laude   Phi Beta Kappa*

RESEARCH INTERESTS:

Emergent Literacy	Children's Literature	Ethnography
Integrated Language Arts	English as a Second Language	Infant Cognition

INTERNATIONAL FELLOWSHIP:

Newman Graduate Fellowship for International Research & Fieldwork, Fall 1998. Collected data and conducted extensive fieldwork regarding early reading programs in central China. Presented seminars, worked with community teams to establish learning centers in rural areas, and collaborated with Nanjing Normal University faculty to develop curricula for practicing teachers.

PUBLICATIONS:

Sampras, A. (1999). <u>Preschool readiness and intercultural expectations</u>. Manuscript submitted for publication.

Sampras, A. (in press). Learning styles and missing the grade. <u>Teacher Magazine</u>.

Sampras, A., Alot, R., & Fine, B.E. (1999). Cognitive abilities and reading strategies of four year olds. <u>Journal of Early Childhood</u>. <u>36</u>, 153-157.

Sampras, A. (1998). Recognizing appropriate learning styles of preschoolers. <u>Journal of Early Childhood</u>. <u>33</u>, 149-151.

Sampras, A., & Goode, B. (1997, October). Developmentally appropriate language arts for preschoolers. <u>Preschool Times</u>, pp. 53-57.

GRADUATE APPOINTMENTS:

Research Assistant, Curriculum and Instruction, UC-Santa Barbara, 1999-present Research, collect, and analyze data for a federally funded project on implications of technology and literacy in southern provinces of China. Work collaboratively with College of Education faculty, State Department, and Minister of Education-Shanghai.

Teaching Assistant, College of Education, UC-Santa Barbara, 1998-1999 Complete responsibility for two sections of Bilingual Methods for Elementary Teachers. Worked closely with students in understanding language acquisition and implementing effective classroom teaching strategies.

TEACHING AND RELATED EXPERIENCES:	**Supervisor - Student Teachers**, Lewis and Clark University, 1994-1995 Observed student teachers, provided feedback and support, and conducted formal three-way conferences among student teacher, college supervisor and cooperating teacher. Organized a regular seminar, evaluated student progress, and assigned grades.

Classroom Teacher, International School of Shanghai, 1992-1994
Prekindergarten teacher (ages 4 to 5). Collaborative setting stressing developmentally appropriate approaches to learning. Worked closely with faculty and student interns from Shanghai International University.

Classroom Teacher, Department of Education, Honolulu, Hawaii, 1990-1992
Bilingual first grade teacher and member of the mentor program.

SERVICE:

Memberships:
National Association for the Education of Young Children
Association for Childhood Education International
International Reading Association
National Council of Teachers of English

Leadership:
Executive Officer (1999- present), Pi Lambda Theta
Chair, Region 10 Education Early Childhood Advisory Council, 1999
Board Member, Idaho Council on Bilingual Education, 1996-1998
President, Pacific Council on Head Start, 1996
Representative, Education Committee, Region 10 Informational Sciences Board, 1996

Consulting:
Bilingual Learning Centers, Inc., Washington D.C.
The Infant Centers, Boise, Idaho; Omaha, Nebraska; Santa Clara, California
University Center for Child Development, Idaho State University
Aerospace Childcare Center, Seattle, Washington

Presentations
"Bilingual Training: Successful Strategies," invited address at Washington State Bilingual Conference, Seattle, May, 1999
"Parent Collaboration in Bilingual Settings," guest speaker, Oakland City Schools Consortium, Oakland, December, 1998
"Technology and Second Language Acquisition," panel member, State Conference on Educational Technology, Los Angeles, March, 1997

LANGUAGES AND TRAVEL:
Fluent in Spanish and Mandarin; Shanghai resident, (8 years)
Advanced Spanish language studies, Mexico City and Madrid Institute,
(4 summers) Rotary Foreign Exchange Student Scholarship, Madrid, Spain, (1 year)

DOSSIER:
Career Development Center, Office of Student Services
Any City, State 12345 Telephone: (101) 555-1000 FAX: (101) 555-1010
Portfolio available for review upon request

Interdisciplinary CV
Strategic Features

- Description of graduate program emphasizes nontraditional preparation and helps the reader to view all experiences from that perspective

- Uncompleted graduate study is listed in Education section because related experiences are included in other sections

- Experience categories accentuate responsibilities at the university level; subheads within the category direct attention to both teaching and research strengths

~

Take a careful look at this sample if

- you need to explain or clarify special features of your graduate program

- your experience includes assistantships or other professional responsibilities in both teaching and research

CHARLOTTE LUCAS

Home: 16 University Avenue
Any City, State 12345
(101) 555-0009

Office: #5 Academic Hall
Any City, State 12345
(101) 555-1111

EDUCATION:

University of Virginia Charlottesville, Virginia	**Ph.D.**	1999-2002	English Education & English

> *Comprehensive Areas:* Contemporary Letters, Emerging Adolescent Literature, Writing
> *Dissertation Topic:* Cultural Perspectives of the Female Adolescent in American
>   Literature Since 1950
> *Dissertation Committee Co-chairs:* Ed U. Cator, Education; Reed A. Lot, English

> *Interdisciplinary doctoral program incorporates courses from the College of Education and the Department of English to examine and to further the relationship between literature and pedagogy. Two committee members have appointments in both departments.*

James Madison University Harrisonburg, Virginia	**M.A.**	1997-1999	American Literature
Clemson University Clemson, South Carolina		1996-1997	Literature
Providence College Providence, Rhode Island	**B.A.**	1989-1992	English Education *with Distinction*

UNIVERSITY EXPERIENCE:

Teaching Experiences

Instructor, University of Virginia, College of Education, 2001-present. Teaching "Introduction to Adolescent Literature" to graduate and undergraduate students. Responsibilities include planning course content, delivering lectures, preparing class reading lists, reviewing and evaluating student performance.

Teaching Assistant, University of Virginia, College of Liberal Arts, English Division, 2000-2001 Responsible for instruction and evaluation of student achievement for two sections of Rhetoric. Maintained regular office hours to work with students on an individual basis.

Research Assistantships

Research Associate, Books for Young Readers Program, University of Virginia, 1999-2000 Assisted in the review of new adolescent literature. Evaluated books, wrote reviews and participated in regular discussion sessions with colleagues and area teachers.

Graduate Research Assistant, Talented and Gifted Center, Clemson University, Spring 1992. Assisted director with summer programs for gifted junior high age girls, and with special projects to encourage gifted female students to pursue interests in sciences and mathematics.

RELATED EXPERIENCE:

Editorial Associate, Scholastic Teen Reading Series, Boston, Massachusetts, 1995-1996
Prepared review and study guide questions for articles and stories dealing with contemporary teen issues; wrote introductions for features and captions for photographs.

Middle School English Teacher, Belmont Public Schools, Belmont, Massachusetts, 1992-1995
Participated in team teaching language arts and reading for grades six through eight, with emphasis on integrated language arts and the writing process.

PUBLICATIONS:

Articles:
　　　　"Frankie and Scout: Nostalgic Narrative Voices," *Virginia English Bulletin* (in press)
　　　　"Eve(ning) in the Garden," *Monday's Daughters*, October 2001
Fiction:
　　　　"The Bees and the Frogs," *GLAD*, June 2000
　　　　"After Math," *Kid Trails*, January 2000
　　　　"The Readers' Club," *The Wanderer*, October 1999
　　　　"Coming to Grips," *Inbound*, Spring 1993
Poetry:
　　　　"Louise," *Kid Trails*, September 2000
　　　　"Returning to Earth," *Young American*, August 18, 1999
　　　　"Chimera, Charisma, Kerygma and Me," *Inbound*, Spring 1995
　　　　"Leading to the Left," *Inbound*, Summer 1994

PROFESSIONAL ACTIVITIES:

"Tomorrow's Poets." Paper presented at the Southeast Language Arts Symposium, Richmond, Virginia. October 2001
Panelist, "The Province of Adolescent Literature," Mid-Atlantic Regional Conference on Gifted Education, Baltimore, Maryland. June 2000
Adjudicator:　　Richmond, Virginia Student Poetry Competition, 2001
　　　　　　　　Fall Writing Fair, Atlantic Council, International Reading Association, 2000
　　　　　　　　South Carolina State High School Poetry Contest, 1999

SCHOLARSHIPS:

Mellow Dissertation Award, Graduate College, University of Virginia, 2001
Graduate Scholar Medallion, James Madison University, 1999
Rita Little Graduate Fellowship in American Literature, Clemson University
Presidential Scholarship (full undergraduate tuition scholarship) Providence College

CREDENTIALS ON FILE:
Office of Student Services, Any City, State 12345 Telephone: (101) 555-1000　FAX: (101) 555-2000

Social Studies Education CV
Strategic Features

- Careful placement of several categories on the first page provides a good overview of teaching, research, and special training

- Works submitted and in progress are carefully stated to give credence to current publishing efforts

- Because presentations are numerous, they are positioned at the end of the CV to allow other categories to be read early

~

Take a careful look at this sample if

- you have several degrees and substantial pre- doctoral experience in research, teaching, and related areas including writing, presentations, etc.

J. JOE BISHOP

21 University Avenue, Any City, State 12345   joe@uiowa.edu   101.555.1000

DEGREES

Ph.D. Candidate: Social Studies Education, The University of Iowa, Iowa City, 1995-present
Dissertation Topic: Conceptions of Democracy and Civic Education in the Czech Republic
Comprehensive Areas: International/ Comparative Education, Language/Culture, Sociology of Culture
M.A. Anthropology, The University of Iowa, 1995
Paper: The Social Context of Representations: An Investigation into the Commentary on the
Mead-Freeman Controversy.
Post-Masters Study, Rhetoric and Communication, University of Oregon, Eugene, 1989-1990
M.A. Sociology, The University of Iowa, 1989
Thesis: Self Referential Behavior in North American Protestant Christianity.
B.A. *cum laude*, Winona State University, Winona, Minnesota, 1987
Majors: Communication Theory & Psychology Minors: Sociology & Mathematics
A.A. *with honors*, Rainy River Community College, International Falls, Minnesota, 1984

RESEARCH AND TEACHING INTERESTS

Research: International and comparative education; social and historical cognition; natural language analysis of academic, educational, religious, and popular culture artifacts and behaviors.
Teaching: Educational anthropology; human relations; educational sociology; comparative and international education; introductory sociology and anthropology; language and culture; knowledge, religion, and popular culture; research methods; social and cultural theory; pedagogy.

SPECIAL TRAINING

Languages: Oral skills: French (fair); Spanish (fair); Czech (basic); Russian (basic); Mongolian (basic)
Reading skills: French (good); Spanish (good); Czech (fair); Russian (basic); Mongolian (functional)
Technology: Webmaster of social studies site (www.uiowa.edu/studies); literate in cross platform software applications; extensive knowledge of specialized software; Internet and WWW resources

FIELD RESEARCH AND INTERNATIONAL EXPERIENCE:

Dissertation fieldwork, August-October 1997, Czech Republic
Civic Education for Czech Republic Project, May 1997, Prague; January 1997- Amsterdam & Prague
French Canadian cultural orientation, June 1992, Québec, Canada

RESEARCH FUNDING OBTAINED

May 1997: T. Anne Cleary International Dissertation Research Award ($800); Dissertation Research
April 1997: Intensive Russian & Czech program & Stanley Foundation ($250): Czech Language Study
March 1993: Office of Academic Affairs ($500): Mongolian language and culture studies
February 1993: Graduate College ($1000): Mongolian language and culture studies
May 1992: Department of Anthropology ($250): Exploratory research in Québec

WORKS SUBMITTED

Bishop, J. Joe, Historical Understanding Among Pre-Service Social Studies Educators: An Examination of the Relationship Between Cognitive Structure and Linguistic Patterns.
Bishop, J. Joe, The Social Context of the Mead-Freeman Controversy

WORKS IN PROGRESS

Bishop, J. Joe, Conceptions of Civic Education and Democracy in the Czech Republic:
An Examination of the Relationship Between Social Position and Cognitive Structure.

WORKING PAPERS

Bishop, J. Joe, Stephen G. Wieting and Anastasia Vogt Yuan. "*Ex ungue leonem*: The Social Context of Honorific Addresses -The Case of the ASA Presidential Speeches."

Bishop, J. Joe, Autopoetic Knowledge Claims Among Protestant Christians: Toward a Theory of Social Complicity.

Bishop, J. Joe, Project INQUIRT: INQUIRy Training for Teachers.

RESEARCH AND TEACHING EXPERIENCE

Adjunct professor: Sociology; Anthropology; Communication, Kirkwood Community College, (1990-)

College supervisor/Czech project coordinator: Student Teachers, University of Iowa (1996-1998)

Test item developer: Iowa Tests of Development, University of Iowa (Summer 1997)

Research assistant: Civic Education-Czech Republic project; University of Iowa (1996-1997)

Teaching assistant: Social Studies Methods, College of Education, University of Iowa (1996)

Teaching assistant: Anthropology Department, University of Iowa (1991-1993)

Research assistant: Program for International Development, University of Iowa (Spring 1991)

Research assistant: National Resource Center on Family Based Services, University of Iowa (1990)

Graduate teaching fellow: Rhetoric and Communication, University of Oregon (1989-1990)

Teaching/research assistant: Sociology Department, University of Iowa (1987-1989)

SELECTED PRESENTATIONS:

Bishop, J. Joe, "Flooded Schools and Environmental Problems in the Czech Republic." First Annual International Day, The University of Iowa, 4 November 1997.

Bishop, J. Joe, "Promoting Social Science Thinking in the Classroom." Iowa Council for the Social Studies Fall, Conference and Workshops. Waterloo, IA, 21 October 1997.

Bishop, J. Joe, "The 'Self-concept' and Reflective Inquiry." Letní skoly:Vychova k obcantsví a demokracii, Olomouc, Czech Republic, 27 August 1997.

Bishop, J. Joe,"Thinking About Democracy: Cognitive Structure and Democratic Action." Letní skoly: Vychova k obcantsví a demokracii Czech Republic, 27 August 1997.

Bishop, J. Joe with Radmila Dostálová, "The Civic Education for the Czech Republic Project and the Didactical Text." Letní skoly: Vychova k obcantsví a demokracii. Czech Republic, August 1997.

Bishop, J. Joe, "Conceptions of Civic Education in the Czech Republic." Policy, Planning, and Leadership Studies Presentation, College of Education, University of Iowa, 22 April 1997.

Bishop, J. Joe, "The Language of Scholarly Controversy." Policy, Planning, and Leadership Studies Brownbag Presentation, College of Education, University of Iowa, December 1995.

Bishop, J. Joe, S. G. Wieting and A. Vogt Yuan, "*Ex ungue leonem*: The Social Context of Production of Sociological Knowledge." Iowa Theory Construction Workshop, University of Iowa, 1995.

Bishop, J. Joe and S. G. Wieting, "The Presidential Standpoint: An Examination of Self-Conceptions of ASA Presidents as a Component of the Social Context of Production of Culture." Paper presentation, Midwest Sociological Society Meetings, Madison, WI, spring 1995.

Bishop, J. Joe 1992 "Samoan Realities: Implications for Knowledge." "Methodological Issues in Ethnography" session, Qualitative Analysis Conference, May 1992, Carlton University, Ottawa.

AFFLIATIONS AND AWARDS (Selected list)

Memberships held in AAA, AERA, NCSS, ASA, ICSS, MSS, CIES, CAE, SSSI, AES

Nominated for life membership - Lambda Alpha; Dean's List; The National Dean's List

Transfer Honors Scholarship; Fine Arts Scholarship,Winona State University

Who's Who in American Junior Colleges; Rainy River Community College Valedictorian

---

Complete CV, writing and research portfolio, and dossier available upon request.

Engineering CV
Strategic Features

- Placing research interests first emphasizes the importance of research in your career

- Concise annotations provide a clear picture of teaching and research responsibilities

- Because publications are numerous, a separate listing is provided

~

Take a careful look at this sample if
- you anticipate an extensive publication record requiring frequent updates

DOUGLAS J. SWENSON

Department of Engineering
#5 Academic Hall
Any City, State 12345
(101) 509-1111

16 University Avenue
Any City, State 12345
(101) 555-0009
djswenson@michtech.edu

RESEARCH INTERESTS
Development and processing of multicomponent materials, correlating chemical reaction kinetics and higher-order phase equilibria with materials properties and processing parameters

EDUCATION

Ph.D., Materials Science (9/94)
University of Wisconsin, Madison, Wisconsin
Thesis: *A Thermodynamic Investigation of Indium-Transition Metal Ohmic Contacts to n-Gallium Arsenide, and an Overview of the Thermochemical Behavior of Quaternary Gallium-Indium-(Transition or Noble Metal)-Arsenic Systems*

M.S., Materials Science (12/88)
University of Wisconsin, Madison, Wisconsin

S.B., Materials Science and Engineering (6/87)
Massachusetts Institute of Technology, Cambridge, Massachusetts

EXPERIENCE

Assistant Professor (8/96-present)
Michigan Technological University, Houghton, Michigan
Department of Metallurgical and Materials Engineering

Thermodynamic modeling and experimental characterization of multicomponent bulk amorphous alloy forming systems
Development of improved electrical contacts to multielemental semiconductors by correlating interfacial chemical reactions with electrical properties
Development of novel self-assembling semiconductor devices through the use of thermodynamic and kinetic principles

Postdoctoral Researcher (10/94-7/96)
Lawrence Livermore National Laboratory, Livermore, California
Metal Processing and Corrosion Section, Chemistry and Materials Science

Developed a novel chemical process for the decarburization of uranium and uranium-base alloys
Planned and directed the experimental determination and thermodynamic modeling of phase equilibria in transition metal-rare earth metal binary systems

EXPERIENCE   Lawrence Livermore National Laboratory (continued)

Performed research and development for multicomponent, titanate-based artificial mineral assemblages for the immobilization of weapons-grade plutonium and uranium

Research Assistant (1988-1991 and 1992-1994)
University of Wisconsin, Madison, Wisconsin
Materials Science Program

Developed $PtIn_2$ ohmic contacts to n-GaAs, correlating contact processing parameters and electrical properties using a novel thermodynamic/kinetic framework

Formulated the groundwork necessary for the development of thermodynamically stable contact materials to $In_xGa_{1-x}As$

Rationalized the electrical behavior and complex metallurgy of In-Ni ohmic contacts to n-GaAs utilizing a detailed thermodynamic analysis of the Ga-In-Ni-As system

SPONSORED
RESEARCH
ACTIVITIES
"Optimization of Glass Forming Ability of Metallic Amorphous Alloys Using Multicomponent Phase Diagram Modeling," National Science Foundation CAREER Program, 1996-1997

"Electronic Materials Processing: Development of Improved Electrical Contacts to Compound Semiconductors and their Alloys," State of Michigan Research Excellence Fund, 1996-1997

ACADEMIC
HONORS
Department of Education Fellowship, 1991-1992
Honorable Mention, National Science Foundation Fellowship, 1988
Wisconsin Alumni Research Foundation Fellowship, 1987-1988
3M Company Prize Fellowship, 1987
Tau Beta Pi, MIT Chapter, 1987
Wisconsin Society for Professional Engineers Scholarship

PROFESSIONAL
ACTIVITIES
Materials Research Society
The Metals, Minerals and Materials Society
ASM International
Sigma Xi
The American Vacuum Society

PUBLICATIONS   Please refer to separate listing

REFERENCES   Available upon request

PUBLICATIONS
Douglas J. Swenson

1.   D. Swenson, S. E. Mohney and Y.A. Chang, "Thermodynamics, Kinetics, and the Design of Contacts to III-V Semiconductors and their Alloys," Invited Review Paper for Mater. Sci. Engin.R, manuscript in progress (1999).

2.   D. Swenson, D. Chen and Y. A. Chang, "Thermodynamically Stable, Ni-Based Ohmic Contacts to n-In$_{0.53}$Ga$_{0.47}$As: A Correlation Between Thermodynamic and Electrical Properties," manuscript in progress, intended for J. Mater. Res. (1999).

3.   D. Swenson, C.-H. Jan, C.-P. Chen and Y. A. Chang, "The Formation of Ohmic and Schottky Enhanced Contacts to III-V Compound Semiconductors *via* an Exchange Mechanism I. A Combined Thermodynamic and Kinetic Model," J. Appl. Phys., submitted (1999).

4.   D. Y. Chen, Y.A. Chang, D. Swenson and F. Shepherd, "Stable Tungsten Ohmic Contacts to n-In$_{0.53}$Ga$_{0.47}$As," J. Mater. Res., in press (1999).

5.   D. Y. Chen, Y. A. Chang and D. Swenson, "Thermally Stable PdIn Ohmic Contacts to n- GaAs via Exchange Mechanism," J. Appl. Phys. **83**, 297 (1998).

6.   D. Swenson, "The Ir$_3$Ge$_7$ (D8$_f$) Structure: An Electron Phase Related to γ-Brass," in Solid-State Chemistry of Inorganic Materials (Eds.: P. Davies, A. Jacobson, C. Torardi and T. Vanderah), Mater. Res. Soc. Symp. Proc. **412** 367 (1997).

7.   D. Swenson, "On the Brass- and Silver-Colored Forms of PtGa$_2$," in Solid-State Chemistry of Inorganic Materials (Eds.: P. Davies, A. Jacobson, C. Torardi and T. Vanderah), Mater. Res. Soc. Symp. Proc. **412** 373 (1997).

8.   D. B. Ingerly, D. Swenson, C.-H. Jan and Y. A. Chang, "Reply to 'Comment on "Phase Equilibria of the Ga-Ni-AS Ternary System,"'" J. Appl. Phys. **82**, 496 (1997).

9.   D. Swenson, T. G. Nieh and J. Fournelle, "The CaO-TiO$_2$-ZrO$_2$ System at 1200°C and the Solubilities of Hf and Gd in Zirconolite," in Scientific Basis for Nuclear Waste Management XIX (Eds.: W. M. Murphy and D. A. Knecht), Mater. Res. Soc. Symp. Proc. **412** 417 (1996).

10. D. Swenson, Sutopo and Y. A. Chang, "Phase Equilibria in the In-Co-As System at 475°C," Mater. Chem. Phys. **44** 215 (1996).

11. D. Swenson and Y. A. Chang, "On the Constitution of Ga-M-P Systems (Where "M" Represents Co, Rh, Ir, Ni or Pt)," Mater. Sci. Engin. **B39** 52 (1996).

Music CV
Strategic Features

- All basic data regarding education, professional experience, and references are on page one

- Principal teachers with significant reputations are identified

- Performance experience augments basic information on first page and is divided into categories; this section could extend to several pages

~

Take a careful look at this sample if

- you have an extensive record of performances or exhibits

- your record of performances or exhibits requires frequent updating

CATHERINE DE BOURGH
16 University Ave
Any City, State 12345
(101) 555-0101 (home)

ACADEMIC PREPARATION

Doctor of Musical Arts, University of Washington, Seattle, Washington, 1999-
Master of Arts in Music, Idaho State University, Pocatello, Idaho, 1990
Bachelor of Music, Seattle Pacific University, Seattle, Washington, 1983

PRINCIPAL TEACHERS

Choral Conducting:	F. M. Elius	Voice: Donna L. Vera
	Chris Johnson	B. F. Pinkerton
	V. Valdee	Floria Tosca

EXPERIENCE

Director of Music, Plymouth Presbyterian Church, Seattle, Washington, June, 1999-
Conduct Senior Choir, an ensemble of 44 voices, and conduct Chapel Choir and
Young People's Choir; soloist for services and special concerts.

Acting Director of Choral Activities, Seattle Pacific University, Seattle, Washington, 1998-1999.
Replaced faculty member on sabbatical leave. Conducted Seattle Pacific University Chorus
Madrigal Singers, a select ensemble of 24 voices, and one community choir. Also taught
classes in first year theory and introductory choral conducting.

Assistant Professor, Choral Conducting, Linfield College, McMinnville, Oregon, 1990-1993.
Conducted Linfield College Choir, an ensemble of 80 voices, and Freshman Chorale, an
ensemble of 36 voices. Taught private voice. Team taught a music appreciation course
for freshmen and sophomores. Soloist, Linfield Faculty Quartet.

Graduate Assistant, Choral Conducting, Idaho State University
Pocatello, Idaho, 1988-1990.
Assistant conductor for the University Chorale, a select ensemble of 32 voices;
soloist, Idaho State Chorus, 1990. European concert tour, 1989.

PROFESSIONAL MEMBERSHIPS

| American Choral Directors Association | Music Educators National Conference |
| College Music Society | National Association of Teachers of Singing |

REFERENCES

Complete dossier available from Career Services and Placement Center
Any City, State 12345 (101) 555-1000

Catherine DeBourgh
Page 2

GUEST CONDUCTING EXPERIENCE

- Northwest Community Chorus Festival, Portland, Oregon. June, 1999
- Washington State High School Music Festival, Seattle, Washington. March, 1999
- University of Washington Music Camp, Seattle, Washington. July, 1998
- Oregon All-State Men's Chorus, Eugene, Oregon. February, 1998
- University of Oregon Music Camp, Eugene, Oregon. July, 1997
- Region XI Honors Choir, Medford, Oregon. April, 1996
- Oregon High School Choral Clinic, Eugene, Oregon. March, 1996

MAJOR WORKS CONDUCTED

Bach, J. S.	*Cantata #4* "Christ lag in Todesbanden"
	Cantata #140 "Wachet Auf"
	Cantata #82 "Ich habe genug"
Brahms, J.	*Ein Deutsches Requiem*
Fauré, G.	*Requiem*
Handel, G.F.	*Messiah* (excerpts)
Haydn, J.	*Kleine Orgelmesse,* "Missa brevis St. Joannis de Deo"
Mozart, W.A.	*Regina Coeli,* K.276
	Exultate, Jubilate
Orff, C.	*Carmina Burana* (excerpts)
Saint-Saëns, C.	*Christmas Oratorio*
Schubert, F.	*Mass in G*
Vivaldi, A.	*Magnificat*

REPRESENTATIVE PERFORMANCES AS VOCAL SOLOIST

Bach, J. S.	*B Minor Mass*
	St. Matthew Passion
Handel, G. F.	*Israel in Egypt*
Haydn, J.	*Harmoniemesse*
Mendelssohn. F.	*Elijah*
Mozart, W. A.	*Requiem*
Stravinsky, I.	*Les Noces*
Vivaldi, A.	*Gloria*

Dental Science CV

Strategic Features

- Degrees are presented first to emphasize advanced preparation in the specific career field

- Short descriptive annotations use action words and specific details to describe teaching and service responsibilities

~

Take a careful look at this sample if

- your degrees are numerous and progressive

- your experience includes assistant-ships and other professional responsibilities in both teaching and research

J. J. Joseph
16 University Avenue, Any City, State 12345
(101) 555-0101 (h) (101) 555-1010 (w)

ACADEMIC BACKGROUND:	M.S.	Orthodontic Residency University of Washington, Seattle	May 1999 (anticipated)
	Certificate	General Practice Residency Veterans Affairs Medical Center Seattle, Washington	July 1997
	D.M.D.	Oregon Health Sciences University School of Dentistry Portland, Oregon	June 1996
	B.S.	Biology, Pacific Lutheran University Tacoma, Washington	May 1993

HONORS:

National Dean's List
Graduated *with highest distinction*
Presidential Citation, Pacific Lutheran University

SPECIAL: RECOGNITION:

American Association of Dental Research Fellowship Recipient, 1998
Dental Research Award Recipient, Washington Dental Society, 1998
Caulk/Dentsply Competion Finalist, 1997
E.I. Wilken Memorial Award, 1997

UNIVERSITY ASSISTANTSHIP:

Teaching Assistant, College of Dentistry, University of Washington,
Fall and Spring, 1998. Faculty advisor: Dr. Karen Northard
Courses: General Histology I, General Histology II, Oral Histology.
Duties included preparation and deliverance of two review sessions
per week and individual tutoring of preprofessional dental students.

EXTERNSHIP/ RELATED COURSEWORK:

Oral Surgery Externship, County Hospital, Seattle, Summer 1998
Anesthesiology, College of Medicine, University of Washington, 1998
Independent Research, Orthodontics, Oregon Health Sciences, 1997
Independent Study, Pediatric Dentistry/Orthodontics, Seattle
       Research Institute, 1997

J.J. Joseph
page 2

RESEARCH AND PRESENTATIONS:	*Research*: Study of Pediatric Dilantin Gingival Hyperplasia *in vitro* *Presentations of research:* Dental Research Conference, Seattle Conference Center, May 9, 1999 Washington Section - International Association for Dental Research Meeting, Vancouver, Washington, March 12, 1998 IADR National Meeting, Los Angeles, California, February 5, 1998
ABSTRACTS:	Joseph, J.J., Meade, K.K. Effects of Pediatric Dilantin Gingival Hyperplasia with Stainless Steel Bands *in vitro,* J Dent Res Special Issue 97, #1897, 1998 Joseph, J.J., Meade, K.K. Effects of Pediatric Dilantin Gingival Hyperplasia *in vitro*, J Dent Res Special Issue 96, #1896, 1998
VOLUNTEER SERVICE:	Migrant Worker Dental Project Participant, Walla Walla County, State of Washington, 1998. Provide dental care to migrant workers and their families in southeastern Washington. Elective Summer Pediatric Rotation Sessions, Bay County Hospital, Seattle, Spring 1997. Worked in a team setting delivering pediatric orthodontic assessment and treatment to indigent patients.
PROFESSIONAL MEMBERSHIPS:	American Dental Association American Association of Dental Schools American Association of Dental Research AADR National Student Research Group Councilor Student Clinicians - American Dental Association (SCADA) (honorary dental society) Psi Omega Dental Fraternity
REFERENCES:	Karen Northard, D.M.D.,Ph.D., University of Washington Zak D. Connell, D.D.S., Ph.D., University of Washington John See-Mann, D.D.S., M.S., Veteran Affairs Medical Center Chriss Gerfishe, Ph.D., Dean of Liberal Arts, Pacific Lutheran

Written references available upon request.
Research abstracts and dental science portfolio available for review.

Creative Writing CV

Strategic Features

- Appropriate terminal degree for creative artist is presented first

- Awards category immediately follows publication record on page one because it recognizes significant achievement

- Readings category with dates and places of invited appearances evidences public interest and recognition of creative work

~

Take a careful look at this sample if

- your work has received prestigious awards or wide recognition

- your professional reputation makes a complete record of all events and activities unnecessary

CHARLES WICKHAM
16 University Avenue, Any City, State 12345
(101) 555-0009

EDUCATION

M.F.A.   English (Creative Writing - Poetry), Arizona State University, Tempe, Arizona, 1999

B.A.   English, Baylor University, Waco, Texas, 1994

TEACHING EXPERIENCE

Assistant Professor, English and Creative Writing, 2000-present
     Southwest Texas State University, San Marcos, Texas
     Teaching responsibilities include two Poetry Workshops, two sections of Modern
     American Poetry, and a seminar: Problems in Modern Poetry. Plan curriculum.
     Lead creative writing workshops. Hold regular individual conferences with students.

Visiting Assistant Professor, Creative Writing, 1999-2000
     Eckerd College, St. Petersburg, Florida
     Taught undergraduate poetry workshops for English majors and two sections of
     lower-division course: Introduction to Reading Poetry. Prepared and delivered
     lectures. Scheduled and coordinated readings by visiting poets.

Teaching Assistant, English Department, 1997-1999
     Arizona State University, Tempe, Arizona
     Teaching responsibilities included: Lyric Poetry (4 sections), Introduction to
     Narrative Literature (two sections), and Interpretation of Literature (two sections).
     Complete responsibility for creating and grading all assignments.

PUBLICATIONS

Third Thoughts, Leontes Publishing (forthcoming)
Expensive Spirit, Leontes Publishing, 2000
Connections: poems of time and place, Androcles Press, 1999
Originally from, chapbook, Endgame Publishing, 1998
Repetitions/reiterations, chapbook, Endgame Publishing, 1998

Poems have appeared in:

Antaeus	Prairie Schooner
Poetry Northwest	Ironwood
Ploughshares	South Florida Poetry Review
The Georgia Review	American Poetry Review
Colorado Review	Gulf Coast

AWARDS

American Academy Poetry Prize, 1999   Arizona Artist Assistance Fellowship, 1998
Ohio University Poetry Prize Finalist, 1999   National Library of Poetry Award, 1998
Rockefeller Foundation Grant, 1999   Southwest Colleges Writers' Award, 1997

READINGS

Live from Prairie Lights, Poetry Reading and live broadcast (WSUI, The University of Iowa
    Radio), Iowa City, Iowa. February 2001
Albuquerque Public Library Poets Series, Albuquerque, New Mexico. January 2001
Texas Book Fair, San Antonio, Texas. October 2000
Young Poets Series, University of Florida, Gainesville, Florida. September 1999
The Writer's Voice, Orlando Arts Council, Orlando, Florida. June 1999
Second Rural Artists Symposium, Colorado Council on the Arts and Humanities,
    Aspen, Colorado. May 1999
Fish Trap Writers Conference, Enterprise, Oregon. February 1999
National Library of Poetry Series, Owings Mills, Maryland. November 1998
Southwest Texas State University, San Marcos, Texas. October 1998
Standing Bear Arts Festival, Tempe, Arizona, August 1998

RELATED EXPERIENCE

Associate Editor, *West Texas Poetry Review,* San Marcos, Texas, 2000-
Reviewer, *South Florida Poetry Review,* Florida Poetry Institute, Miami, Florida, 1999-2000
Poetry Editor, *ASU Poetry Review,* Arizona State University, 1998-1999
Contributing Editor, *words worth review,* Santa Clara, California, 1997-1998
Editor, *Earthmarks* (undergraduate literary magazine), Baylor University, 1992-1994

Editorial responsibilities included selecting work for publication, editing and
proofreading copy, writing press releases and designing press packages,
developing special programs, and serving as liaison to authors, editors,
publishers, and subscribers. Supervised staff, interns, and volunteers.

DOSSIER

Education Placement Office, Any City, State 12345
Phone: (101) 555-1000   FAX: (101) 555-2000

Modern Language CV
Strategic Features

- Undergraduate degree is listed first for applications to similar colleges

- To emphasize the diversity of institutions attended, college names are listed before dates of attendance, degrees, or courses of study

- Teaching interests are listed to emphasize breadth of background and preparation

~

Take a careful look at this sample if

- you are in the early stages of a degree program

- you need to describe specific professional responsibilities

MARGUERITE LAROQUE

16 University Avenue   #5 Academic Hall
Any City, State 12345   Any City, State 12345
(101) 555-0101   (101) 555-1010

ACADEMIC PREPARATION

Luther College, Decorah, Iowa   Bachelor of Arts, French & English,
                                                  1992-1996

Institute of European Studies, Nantes, France   Certificât, French Language, 1996

University of Michigan, Ann Arbor, Michigan   Master of Arts, English, 1996-1998

Stanford University, Stanford, California,   Doctor of Philosophy, French, 1998-
       Course work and comprehensive exams to be completed July 2000

TEACHING INTERESTS

French Language & Culture   Francophone Literature
Twentieth Century French Literature   Rhetoric

EXPERIENCE

Teaching Assistant, General Education Courses - Literature, University of Michigan, 1996-1998
Complete responsibility for teaching two courses: Interpretation of Literature and American
Lives. Prepared and delivered lectures, designed exams and evaluated students' progress.
Additional responsibilities included curriculum review and course revision.

Teaching Assistant, French Department, Stanford University, 1998-2000
Complete responsibility for instruction and grading of introductory language course stressing
development of oral and written communication skills. Maintained regular office hours to
 advise and assist students.

ACADEMIC HONORS

Graduated cum laude   Julian Senior Scholarship, 1996
Dean's List, six semesters   Leeman Graduate Fellowship Award, 1998

PROFESSIONAL MEMBERSHIPS

Modern Language Association   American Association of Teachers of French
Southwest Modern Language Association   Women's Caucus for the Modern Languages

DOSSIER

Student Services Center, Any City, State 12345 Telephone: (101)555-1000 FAX: (101)555-2000

Accounting CV
Strategic Features

- Because the Ph.D. is not completed, dissertation topic is indicated to show progress; thesis title and advisor for the M.A. degree are also listed to emphasize commitment to research and academic pursuits

- Research is emphasized on the first page; theoretical and practical experiences are indicated

- To avoid redundancies, Teaching Experience category has one combined description covering both assistantships

~

Take a careful look at this sample if

- you have an interest in presenting both research and teaching interests

AMANDA J. BROWN

Accounting Department   21 University Avenue
The University of Michigan   Any City, State 12345
Ann Arbor, Michigan 12344   aj-brown@umich.edu
001.111.1234 (w)   101.555.1000 (h)

EDUCATION:	THE UNIVERSITY OF MICHIGAN, Ann Arbor, Michigan
	Ph.D. Candidate in Accounting, May 2000
	Dissertation Topic: Valuation and Reporting
	Dissertation Chair: Donald Smith, Ph.D.
	THE OHIO STATE UNIVERSITY, Columbus, Ohio
	M.S. Accounting, May 1996
	Thesis: Audit Decision-Making Models
	Advisor: Monte Dolar, Ph.D.
	UNIVERSITY OF CHICAGO, Chicago, Illinois
	B.S. Statistics, May 1992 *cum laude*
TEACHING INTERESTS:	Cost accounting
	Corporate financial reporting
RESEARCH INTERESTS:	Regulation and financial analysis models
	Accounting information systems
RESEARCH EXPERIENCE:	Research Assistant, Accounting Department,
	The University of Michigan, 1997 - 1998
	Responsibilities in above research assistantship included:

- Designed and completed survey of 200 corporations to analyze valuation of corporate financial reporting systems.
- Developed statistical model using SAS to determine correlation factors.
- Completed index to published textbook on cost accounting.

RESEARCH RELATED EMPLOYMENT:

Statistical Analyst, Federal Reserve Bank of Chicago, 6/92 -7/94
- Assigned to provide background analyses and reports to region banks.
- Examined initial computer reports to determine accuracy

TEACHING EXPERIENCE:	Teaching Assistant, Accounting Department, The University of Michigan, September 1996 - present Graduate Assistant, Department of Accounting, The Ohio State University, August 1994 - May 1996 Responsibilities in above teaching assistantships included

TEACHING
EXPERIENCE:

Teaching Assistant, Accounting Department,
The University of Michigan, September 1996 - present
Graduate Assistant, Department of Accounting,
The Ohio State University, August 1994 - May 1996
Responsibilities in above teaching assistantships included

- Conducted lecture and recitation sessions for two classes per semester including Principles of Accounting, Cost Accounting, and Financial Accounting.
- Graded exams and case studies for up to 120 students per course (graduate and undergraduate students)
- Received outstanding student evaluations with an average of 5.62 on a 6- point scale.

PRESENTATIONS:

"Information Systems: Analyzing the Profit Margin,"
presentation at the Regional Meeting of Association of
Accounting Professionals, Seattle, October, 1997

WORKS IN
PROGRESS:

The Role of Valuation Models in Corporate Financial
Restructuring" with Susan Pommer
Information Systems: An Analysis of Cost and Benefits to
Audit Managers" with Donald Smith

COMPUTER
SKILLS:

Statistical Programs: SAS, SPSSx, SPSS/PC
Spreadsheet/database software: Access, Excel, Lotus Notes,
Generalized Audit

HONORS:

John H. Meyer Award for Excellence, 1998
Big Ten Doctoral Consortium Fellow, 1997
Cited for top quartile of teaching evaluations, 1996 - 1998
Outstanding Teaching Assistant Award, 1996
Passed CPA Exam, 1995, Ohio

PROFESSIONAL
MEMBERSHIPS:

American Accounting Association
American Institute of Certified Public Accountants
Institute of Management Accountants

REFERENCES:

Available Upon Request

MBA CV

Strategic Features

- Degrees and teaching interests are listed early to give focus to the CV and to highlight the dual areas of academic preparation

- Graduate assistantships are annotated to provide an overview of the supervisory and instructional responsibilities involved in the three positions

- Page two provides relevant intern and professional employment experiences with annotations describing the varies responsibilities involved in both settings

∼

Take a careful look at this sample if

- you have a dual degree with two job interests (compare with the one-page law résumé on page 117)

JAMES J. HUBERTY
21 University Ave, Any City, State 12345
jj@uiowa.edu   101.555.1010

DEGREES

The University of Iowa, Iowa City, Iowa

Master in Business Administration and Juris Doctor, May 1998

Honors:	School of Management Graduate Fellowship
	College of Law Scholar Tuition Scholarship
Activities:	Student Marketing Association Member
	Honor and Ethics Code Committee Member

Bachelor of Science Degree in Business Administration, May 1991

Majors:	Finance and Marketing
Honors:	Graduated *with distinction*
	Dean's List six consecutive semesters
	University of Iowa Honors Scholarship
	University of Iowa Tuition Scholarship
	Maytag Corporation Scholarship
	Melville Corporation Scholarship

TEACHING AND RESEARCH INTERESTS

Introduction to law, managerial finance, strategic management and business policy; managerial economics, corporate financial reporting, marketing management, management of technology transfer, data product design, development, and decisions.

GRADUATE ASSISTANTSHIPS: THE UNIVERSITY OF IOWA

Teaching Assistant Supervisor - Introduction to Law, College of Business Administration, 8/96 - 5/98
- Coordinate and direct four graduate-level teaching assistants in *Introduction to Law* course.
- Responsible for creation, organization, and construction of exam questions and assignments.
- Meet regularly with faculty to evaluate curricula and performance of graduate teaching assistants.

Teaching Assistant - Introduction to Law, College of Business Administration, 8/95 - 5/98
- Prepare and present course material to undergraduate classes and lead class discussions. Discussions focus on defining legal rules and principles, and illuminating their rationale.
- Create teaching materials, design test items, and track student results using self-designed computer applications using databases, spreadsheets, wordprocessing and the Internet.
- Designed database to manage administrative tasks including grading, enrollment and attendance for approximately 100 undergraduate students.

Legal Research Assistant, College of Law, Summer 1995
- Researched case law and academic journals regarding civil forfeiture and its legality considering the implications of the Double Jeopardy Clause.
- Worked closely with Professors L.G. Galloe and Mary Jorgensen in drafting and editing manuscript materials for various publications.
- Assisted in the planning and organization of a regional law conference involving students, scholars, and legal experts in the field.

PROFESSIONAL EMPLOYMENT AND SERVICE
James J. Huberty, page 2

LAW INTERNSHIP
Lord, Bissell & Brook, Chicago, Illinois
Summer Associate, May 1997 - August 1997
Worked as an intern in Lord, Bissell & Brook, a firm of 99 partners and 145 associates
specializing in insurance, litigation, and corporate law. Specific intern responsibilities included:
- Extensive research performed regarding a variety of legal issues.
- Drafted legal memoranda for internal and external use.
- Named a contributing author to client newsletter.
- Worked closely with firm members in several different departments.

PROFESSIONAL EMPLOYMENT
Old Republic Asset Management Corporation, Chicago, Illinois
Investment Analyst, April 1992 - August 1994
Assisted Corporate Investment Officer/Portfolio Manager in management of approximately
$2.5 billion asset portfolio. Evaluated investment opportunities and provided reports
regarding the status and makeup of the investment portfolios under management;
conducted extensive communication and trading activity and institutional brokerage
services; created and maintained portfolio database reports to be utilized for corporate and
strategic management purposes.
Specific responsibilities included:
- *Cash management:* Transferred and invested short-term funds in accordance with corporate
  cash flow needs including issuance & redemption of Commercial Paper (paper
  outstanding $40-$70 million)
- *Securities transactions:* Purchased and sold high grade equity and fixed income
  securities for corporate accounts. Transactions were of large-block nature and were
  executed through institutional brokerage services. Market timing and sensitivity to the
  effects of large-block trading on market prices were of primary importance.
- *Investment research:* Located and evaluated investment opportunities through the use of
  on-line database services, brokerage reports, and other institutional services. Utilized resources
  for evaluating existing portfolio holdings.
- *Analysis:* Analyzed potential and currently held securities for the appropriateness of inclusion
  within corporate portfolios; conducted credit, market, and financial statement analysis,
  maturity matching and other analytic methodologies. Made recommendations to the Portfolio
  Manager and the Executive Officer for consideration.
- *CFA candidate:* Sat for and passed first of three examinations for Chartered Financial Analyst
  designation.

SERVICE AND PROFESSIONAL DEVELOPMENT
Service:
Writing Center Tutor, University of Iowa Law School, 1996 - 1998
Volunteer leadership positions, Student Marketing Association, 1996 - 1997

Professional Development Seminars and Presentations:
Diversity in Law: Race and Gender Issues Seminar, October, 1997
Speaker Series on Tax Revisions for the Coming Mulliumn, Spring, 1998

References and writing sample provided upon request.

Fine Arts CV

Strategic Features

- Simple graphic frames candidate's address

- Category headings at left margin give flexibility in arranging information

- Principal teachers are highlighted to indicate study with acknowledged masters

- Exhibitions divided by classification provide evidence of recognition as productive artist

~

Take a careful look at this sample if

- your objective is a faculty position but your current experience is outside academe

CLIFFORD HEATH

| 16 University Avenue | Any City, State 12345 | (101) 555-0101 |

EDUCATION

M.F.A. Studio Art
University of Illinois at Urbana-Champaign, 1999

B.A. Studio Art
Kansas City Art Institute, Kansas City, Missouri, 1994

TEACHING
INTERESTS

Ceramics (beginning to advanced)
Sculpture
3D Design

TEACHING
EXPERIENCE

Teaching Assistant
    University of Illinois Ceramics Studio, 1997-99
Ceramics Instructor
    University Memorial Union Craft Center, 1997-99
Ceramics Instructor
    Champaign Cultural Center, 1997-98

CURRENT
EMPLOYMENT

Private teaching, operate ceramics studio/supply shop
Self-employed in ceramics production

RELATED
EXPERIENCE

Graphic Artist, American College Testing
    Iowa City, Iowa, 1994-1996
Matting and Framing, Contemporary Art Supplies
    Chicago, Illinois, 1990-1994 (summers)

INVITATIONAL
EXHIBITIONS

Ceramic Revelations, Hickock Memorial Gallery
    Jefferson City, Missouri (June-August, 2000)
Grandeis Artspace 4th Annual Exhibit, 2000
    Grand Rapids, Michigan
Form/al/ities in Three Dimensions, 1999
    Racine Fine Arts Center, Racine, Wisconsin
Iowa Sculpture Invitational, 1999
    Blanden Gallery, Fort Dodge, Iowa
Middlemarch Gallery Invitational Ceramics Exhibit, 1999
    Muncie, Indiana
Contemporary Ceramics Invitational, 1998
    Cooper Gallery, Cleveland, Ohio

Clifford Heath
Page Two

JURIED
SHOWS

1999 to Present
First Place, Kansas City Artists Exhibit 2001, Kansas City
Art Gallery, Kansas City, Missouri
Purchase Prize, Missouri Clay and Paper Regional Show
St. Louis, Missouri
Second Prize, Illinois Ceramic & Sculpture Show
Springfield, Illinois
30th Annual Ceramic Artists' Show, Omaha Fine
Arts Center, Omaha, Nebraska
Mid-Mississippi Annual Exhibition, Quad Cities Arts
Center, Davenport, Iowa
Pheasant Run Ceramics Show
Elgin, Illinois
Clearwater Artists and Artisans
Grand Rapids, Michigan

GROUP
SHOWS

Form Follows, Functional Ceramics, 1999
Webster Gallery, Skokie, Illinois
University of Illinois Graduate Student Show, 1998
University of Illinois Gallery
Ceramic Celebrations, Bryant Gallery, 1998
Highland Park, Illinois
New Horizons Art Show, 1998
Chicago Public Library
Iowa Ceramic Arts Exhibit, 1997
Cedar Rapids Arts Center
Summer Arts Fair, Montana State University, 1996
Bozeman, Montana
Contemporary Ceramicists, Rolling Hills Center, 1996
Shawano, Wisconsin

PROFESSIONAL
MEMBERSHIPS

College Art Association
Midwest Ceramics Association
Illinois Sculptors' Association

DOSSIER

Education Placement Center
Any City, State 12345
Phone (101) 555-1000
FAX (101) 555-1010

History CV

Strategic Features

- First page conveys a quick professional overview; could be used in any situation calling for a CV

- Page 2 contains recent and selected professional activities

- Categories on page 2 can be expanded, rearranged, or modified to suit various purposes

~

Take a careful look at this sample if

- your extensive professional abilities and achievements are not directly related to your immediate goal, i.e., moving into central administration

CAROLINE BINGLEY
#5 Academic Hall, Any City, State 12345
(101) 555-1111

FORMAL EDUCATION

Syracuse University	M.A. 1979; Ph.D. 1984	History
Vassar College	A. B. 1977	History & French

TEACHING OVERVIEW

University of North Carolina,	Professor	1993-present
Chapel Hill	Associate Professor	1989-1993
	Assistant Professor	1986-1989
University of Paris (Institut d'Anglais)	Visiting Professor	Fall 1987
New York University	Instructor	1984-1986
Syracuse University	Teaching Assistant	1979-1981
	Research Assistant	1981-1984

ADMINISTRATIVE EXPERIENCE

Chair, Department of Women's Studies, 1995-present
Acting Assistant Dean, College of Arts & Letters, 1993-1995
Chair, University of North Carolina's Human Rights Board, 1990-1993
Co-Chair, Governor's Educational Review Board, 1988-1991

PUBLICATIONS

BOOKS:
European Women in the 17th Century, University Press, Los Angeles, 1996.
Women's Influence in the Intellectual Society: Case Studies from the Seventeenth Century, Oxford
        University Press, London, 1990. (co-author with Egan Dewitt, Ph.D.)
Women and the Working Class: 1550-1600, Marquis Publishing, Ltd., London, 1987.

ARTICLES:
A total of 76 articles have been published. Articles published since 1997 are listed below.
"Feminism in Eighteenth Century France," *Socialist Women,* 3, 2 (Fall 1998): 39-58.
"Feminism and the Family," *Women's Studies Quarterly,* 4, 8 (October 1998): 117-131.
"Men and Role-Reversal: 1600-1650," *Journal of Interdisciplinary History,* IX, 3 (Fall 1997): 28-46.
"Diaries of 17th Century Feminist Workers," *Socialist Women,* 2, 1 (Spring 1997): 12-21.
"Women in the Workplace: Textile Workers' Conditions in the 1600's," *Journal of Social History,* 25, 2
        (February 1997): 77-93.

TRANSLATIONS:
"Turn of the Century Higher Education: Women's Studies in France," *Women's Studies Quarterly,*
        International Supplement 3 (September 1993): 22-30.
"The Family and Feminism," translations of Chloé Millet's "La famille et le feminisme," *French
        American Review,* VI, 4 (Spring 1991): 89-100.

BOOK REVIEWS:

The Women's Review of Books	*American Historical Review*
Journal of Social History	*Los Angeles Times Book Review*

CONFERENCE PRESENTATIONS

PAPERS PRESENTED, 1995-present:

"History of Women's Experiences in Seventeenth Century France," Society for French Historical Studies, University of Minnesota, March 1998. (Invited).

"Population and Activism," American Historical Association, Chicago, May 1997.

"Learning from Sacrifice: Women in the 1600's," Western Association of Women Historians, Mills College, June 1996. "Ten Reasons Why Women's Studies Works," Berkshire Conference on the History of Women, Lesley College, January 1995.

GRANTS, FELLOWSHIPS, AND OTHER AWARDS

Outstanding Teaching Award, 1998

National Endowment for the Humanities, Senior Nominee, 1998

Rockefeller Foundation Research Grant, 1997

American Philosophical Society Summer Fellow, 1996

National Science Foundation, Scientific Personnel Improvement Division, 1995-96

Harvard University Mellon Faculty Summer Humanities Fellowship, 1992

Summer Research Fellowship, Stanford University, 1987, 1991

Ford Foundation Dissertation Fellowship, 1978-1979

UNIVERSITY SERVICE

Chair, University Recruitment Committee, 1998-present

Member, Scholarship Fund Committee, 1995; Chair, 1997-present

Chair, Search Committee for Vice President of Research, 1996

Chair, Promotion and Tenure Committee, 1994-96

Member, Board of Directors, University Foundation, 1994-1995

Senate Member, University Faculty Senate, 1992-1994

Faculty Member, Board of Control of Athletics, 1990-1994

Member, Honors Committee, 1988

OUTREACH

Speaker, consultant or panel participant for numerous events and organizations at the local, state and regional level. Guest speaker for public radio and cable TV news specials.

Recent consulting at the following institutions:

Boston University	Lesley College
New Mexico State University	St. Olaf College
Notre Dame University	St. Mary's College
University of Arizona	Indiana University
Queen's University	Stetson University

DOSSIER AVAILABLE UPON REQUEST

Library/Media CV
Strategic Features

- Career Overview and Professional Skills categories are listed early to demonstrate progressive responsibilities and qualifications

- Academic Service and Leadership categories evidence commitment and peer respect on campus and in professional associations

- Concise annotations provide comprehensive career profile

~

Take a careful look at this sample if

- you are seeking an administrative or service position

- your professional and collegial activities are extensive and significant

WILLIAM COLLINS

16 University Avenue, Any City, State 12345   (101) 555-0101 (home)

EDUCATION	Ph.D.	Instructional Design and Technology, 1999-present Northwestern University, Evanston, Illinois
	M.A.	Library Science, 1993 University of Wisconsin-Madison, Madison, Wisconsin
	B.S.	Computer Science, 1988 University of Wisconsin-Superior, Superior, Wisconsin

CAREER OVERVIEW

Media Administrator	5 years
Reference Librarian	5 years
Computer Programmer	4 years

PROFESSIONAL SKILLS

- Administer comprehensive media services
- Develop and manage budgets
- Establish operational policies
- Supervise, train and evaluate professional staff members
- Utilize technology and current research methods

RELATED EXPERIENCE

Director - Media Services, 2000-present
Associate Director - Library and Media Services, 1997-2000
Marquette University, Milwaukee, Wisconsin

Reference Librarian, 1993-1997
University of Wisconsin-Parkside, Kenosha, Wisconsin

Computer Programmer, 1989-1993
Claims Division, Classified Insurance Co., Milwaukee, Wisconsin

ACADEMIC SERVICE

Chair, Technology Committee, Marquette University, 2000-present
Coordinate activities and responsibilities of committee; assess
current technology on campus; project needs and evaluate
emerging technology.

Adviser, Technology Student Association, Marquette University,
2000-present
Assist students in organizing a campus chapter; counsel students
regarding by-laws, membership requirements, etc.

William Collins
Page 2

ACADEMIC SERVICE
(continued)

Acting Media Services Department Chair, University of Wisconsin-Parkside, 1999-2000
Responsible for budget preparation, performance evaluations and course scheduling.

Committee Work
1995-present
Served on and chaired numerous committees ranging from technology, staff development, institutional advisory, reaccreditation, to faculty and staff searches.

LEADERSHIP

President, Staff Council, Marquette University, 2000-2001
Governed decision-making body of the professional staff; provided liaison between staff and the administration.

Executive Board Member, Library and Information Technology Association, 1998-present. Chaired technology division, coordinated policy review meetings; acted as representative for regional associations.

President, Great Lakes Association for Communication Technology, 1996-1998. Conducted all executive board and general membership meetings, supervised business transactions, and initiated extensive membership drives.

PROFESSIONAL ACTIVITIES

Co-chair, Legislative Task Force on Higher Education
Member, Wisconsin Legislative Committee on Technology
Committee Member, Department of Education Higher Education Task Force
Wisconsin Delegate, Association for Educational Communications and Technology
Board of Directors, United Way of Milwaukee

MEMBERSHIPS

Great Lakes Association for Communication Technology
Library and Information Technology Association
Association for Educational Communications and Technology
Wisconsin Association for Communication Technology
Midwest Higher Education Instructional Resources Consortium

Dossier available at Education Placement and Career Services
Any City, State 12345
(101) 555-1000   FAX: (101) 555-2000

School Administration CV

Strategic Features

- Degrees are presented first to show completion of terminal degree appropriate for college faculty positions

- For purposes of introduction (not related to employment), the first page of the CV could be used alone

- Page two provides a comprehensive and useful summary of leadership and professional service that can be expanded easily to accommodate new material

~

Take a careful look at experience with different this sample if

- you have substantial responsibilities

- it is to your advantage to highlight recent or selected activities

A. J. BARE

16 Ridge Drive   Any City, State 12345   (101) 555-1010   aj-bare@cgs.edu

ACADEMIC PREPARATION

Ph.D.   Policy and Leadership Studies, May 1999, Claremont Graduate School, California, 1999
Dissertation: Cultural Comparisons of Urban Education: A Case Study of Romanian Urban Youth and Los Angeles Urban Youth, Advisor-Bea Fine, Ph.D.

M.A.   Educational Administration, May 1992, Rice University, Houston, Texas
Thesis: Interdisciplinary Models: Urban Schools That Succeed, Advisor-Will B. Goode

B.S.   German Studies and History, 1985, Texas A&M University, College Station, Texas
with highest honors

TEACHING AND RESEARCH INTERESTS

Interdisciplinary Approaches to Administration
Education and International Development
Politics & Economics in Urban Education

School Organizational Patterns
Financial Management
Contemporary Management Theory

UNIVERSITY LEVEL EXPERIENCE

Graduate Research Assistant, Policy Leadership Studies, Claremont Graduate School, 1998.
Under the direction of Professor Reed A. Lott, collected, reviewed, and analyzed the early school restructuring movement. Developed a bibliography for use in the course *School Reformation*. Bibliography incorporated into the index of the *Policy Leadership Handbook* edited by Dr. Lott.

Fulbright Scholar Program-Research Award, Bucharest, Romania, 1998-1999. In consultation with Romanian education officials studied school curricula and state-mandated materials with a special emphasis on technology. Reviewed government archives and worked closely with Romanian post-secondary instructors to examine curriculum resources.

West Coast Educational Consortium Grant, National Coalition for Urban Youth, 1998-present.
In collaboration with Claremont faculty, awarded grant ($550,000) to initiate urban learning centers. Working in cooperation with state education leaders, teachers, business and community leaders to design centers that prepare urban students for workforce success.

K - 12 EXPERIENCE

Superintendent of Schools, Santa Monica-Malibu USD, Santa Monica, California, 1995-1998
Enrollment and staff: 12,900 students, 545 certified staff, 200 non-certified staff, 38 administrators
Budget: 100.4 million; successful bond referendum: 18.8 million for new year-round high school

Assistant Superintendent, 1992-1995; High School Principal, 1990-1992; Assistant High School Principal, 1989-1990, Riverside Public Schools, Riverside, California

Classroom Teacher, German and History, 1985- 1989. Clark County Schools, Las Vegas, Nevada (2 years); Edgewood Independent School Disrict, San Antonio, Texas (3 years)

A. J. BARE

PROFESSIONAL SERVICE
(1996 - present)

Leadership:
Representative, California Governor's Commission on Secondary and Middle Schools, 1999-present.
Conference Chair, Western Regional Educational Association, Los Angeles, October 15-16, 1999.
Board Member, State of California Economic Development Growth Commission, 1997-1998.
President (1997) and charter member, Urban Schools Coalition, Los Angeles County, 1996-present.

Presentations:
"Restructuring =Total Commitment," State Governor's Forum, Oakland, California, March 1999.
"Involving Parents in School Programs," School Administrators Conference, Stanford, May 1999.
"Partnerships with Real Results," American School Administrators Meeting, Atlanta, October 1998.
"Telecommunications: Tools for Reform," Southwest School Boards Conference, Phoenix, 1997.
"Global Communities and Learning Initiatives," New Schools Coalition Meeting, Detroit, July 1997.
"Designing Schools for Success," National Education Association Convention, Detroit, April 1997.
"Technology and Urban School Reform," NEA National Conference Series, Tampa, June 1996.

Publications:
Bare, A.J. and Dunne, I.M. "Demystifying Reform," *Learning Magazine,* 4, 2 (May 1999): 17.
Bare, A.J. "One Approach to School Reform," *West Curriculum Bulletin,* XI, 3 (Fall 1998): 7-9.

Partnerships and Grants:
Technology Grant, West Coast Partnership Inc., Los Angeles, California, 1997- 1999. Working in partnership with staff, university and local corporate leaders in developing state-of-the-art technology labs in K-12 buildings. Designing a shared professionals exchange to utilize the expertise of business leaders in classrooms; teachers provide enrichment courses at business site.

Coastal Project Block Grant, Los Angeles County Business School Partnership, 1997. Initiated and led the design and development of two new urban learning centers that incorporate performance-based learning goals; year-round, evening and flexible hours; integrated coursework; technology infusion; teaching teams and community advisory boards.

Memberships:

American Association of School Administrators	New Schools Coalition
California Association of School Administrators	National Education Association
West Coast Regional Association	National Alliance of Black Educators

Community Activism:
Commission member, Youth 2000, Los Angeles County; Elected to Board of Directors, 1999
President (1998) and member of Southern California Youth Action Committee, 1996 - present
Chair, Chamber of Commerce Futures Committee, Los Angeles Chamber of Commerce, 1996 -1998
Volunteer Big Brother, Southside Los Angeles Big Brother, Inc., 1995 - present

Dossier available at Educational Career Services, Any City, State 12345   (101) 555-1000

Counseling CV
Strategic Features

- First three categories present comprehensive overview of expertise, progressive experience and degrees

- Responsibilities of each professional position are briefly annotated to show breadth of experiences and responsibilities

- To condense CV to two pages, some categories represent only selected or most recent activities

~

Take a careful look at this sample if

- you have several years of progressive professional experience

- you have a number of professional activities, i.e. publications, speeches, service; a complete documentation of activities may require several pages.

MIA S. AMPLE

16 University Ave, Any City, State 12345

(101) 555-1010 (office)   mia-ample@umaine.edu

AREAS OF EXPERTISE	Research Techniques in Male-Dominated Cultures Vocational Psychology Behavioral Counseling and Psychotherapy Clinical Assessment and Measurement

EXPERIENCE SUMMARY	Associate Professor	two years
	Counseling Center Director	three years
	Assistant Professor	five years
	Staff Counselor	two years

DEGREES	Ph.D.	Counseling Psychology 1994 Columbia University, New York
	M.A.	Counseling and Human Development 1987 Washington University, St. Louis, Missouri
	B.A.	Classics 1985 Pepperdine University, Malibu, California

CURRENT EXPERIENCE

Associate Professor (1998-present), Assistant Professor (1994-1998)
College of Education, Department of Counseling and Psychology
University of Maine, Bangor, Maine
Responsible for teaching and program development in master's and doctoral degree programs in counseling psychology. Coordinate and supervise entry-level community-based practica. Teaching responsibilities include core courses in educational psychology, mental health services, and educational psychology.

Director, Counseling Center (1997-present)
University of Maine, Bangor, Maine
Responsible for budget design and maintenance, staffing, policies and procedures, and evaluation of the 12-member counseling staff.

RELATED PROFESSIONAL EXPERIENCE

Fulbright Scholar, Morocco, 1997; Ford Foundation Award, Jordan, 1995
Examined employment factors and incidences of depression in unemployed young adult males with no formal education or job training.

Staff Counselor, Counseling Center
Lincoln University, Jefferson City, Missouri (1987-1990)
Coordinated career program development component. Responsibilities included counseling and psychological evaluations for undergraduates.

MIA S. AMPLE
Page 2

CURRENT
PROFESSIONAL
SERVICE

Chair, Graduate Admissions Council, University of Maine, 1999-
University of Maine Grievance Committee Member, 1998-
Search Committee Chair, University Counseling Center Counselor, 1998
Member, University Technology Advisory Board, 1997-1998
Editorial Consultant, Higher Education Series, Jossey-Bass, Inc., 1997
Consultant, STAR Program, U.S. Department of Education, 1995-1997

SELECTED
PUBLICATIONS

Handbook on Rehabilitation Programs for the Disabled, by Mia Ample,
Alan Publishing House, New York, (forthcoming, 1999).
"The Realities of Rehabilitation Centers," by Mia Ample and Alec Salle,
Rehabilitation Counseling Bulletin, 1992, Vol 57.
"Interview Techniques for Rehabilitation Counselors," by Mia Ample,
Journal of Applied Rehabilitation Counseling, October, 1990, Vol 63, No.2.
"Inservice Training for Campus-based Counseling Centers," by Mia
Ample, *The Personnel and Guidance Journal*, June, 1990, Vol 5.

MAJOR
ADDRESSES
(since 1997-)

"The Changing Role in Counseling Centers," American Personnel and
Guidance Association National Convention, Chicago, April, 1999.
"Interview Behavior and Client Outcome," Western Association for
Counselor Education and Supervision Conference, Detroit, May, 1998.
"Therapy and the Role of the Family," Changing Family Conference IX,
The University of Iowa, Iowa City, February, 1997.

AFFILIATIONS

American Education Research Association
National Rehabilitation Association
American Rehabilitation Counseling Association
American Personnel and Guidance Association
American Association of University Professors

SPECIAL
DISTINCTIONS

Awarded Outstanding Teacher Award, University of Maine, 1998
Fulbright Award, Summer 1998, Rabat, Morocco
Ford Foundation Fellowship, 1994-1995 Amman, Jordan
Phi Beta Kappa; Magna Cum Laude

LICENSURE

Board Certification- psychologist, Maine, California
Certified consulting psychologist, Missouri State Board of Psychology

Dossier available at Placement Center, Any City, State 12345 (101)555-1000

Tailoring Your CV

Conceptualizing, selecting information, categorizing, arranging, rearranging, through draft after draft, takes anywhere from a few hours to several weeks. Even after all this effort, you may discover that your carefully polished and refined CV is not appropriate for all opportunities or in all situations.

Institutions vary in their mission, their focus, their goals. Because of these differences, your CV should be tailored to fit the institution. For example, community colleges and undergraduate institutions will be primarily interested in your teaching abilities. Universities tend to place greater emphasis on research and scholarly capabilities and will look for evidence of your achievement or potential in these areas.

Teaching Emphasis

If you know that the primary mission of the institution is undergraduate education at or below the baccalaureate level, you will want to focus on:

- teaching experience
- teaching interests
- qualifications as a generalist

- student contact, especially with lower division students
- experience or attendance at similar institutions
- pedagogical training and licensure (if applicable)

Research Emphasis

Institutions with graduate or professional programs may also place considerable emphasis on teaching ability. In addition, such institutions are likely to value:

- scholarly productivity
- research interests
- research experience
- field or laboratory experience
- areas of specialization
- technical expertise
- grant writing or other development activities
- contact or collaboration with recognized authorities in the field

Adapt your information to the intended audience. A CV that does not seem appropriate for the place or the position will not be taken seriously by potential employers. Take the time to prepare a CV that focuses attention on the characteristics, the experiences, and the potential that will be of greatest interest to the selection committee.

International Version

Adapting your CV for faculty positions in international settings requires only minor adjustments. State and federal hiring guidelines regarding equal employment opportunities without regard to age, gender, religious affiliation, race or ethnicity are not relevant outside the United States. For applications outside the United States, some of this information may be requested or even required by hiring officials.

The principal addition to your CV concerns information about your citizenship and possibly selected personal data. Because of visa requirements, housing availability, and travel allowances, your CV should include information about anyone who will accompany you (spouse, partner, dependents).

Language competencies can be an important consideration, even if they do not reflect the language of the host country. Colleges and universities will indicate if the language of instruction is English, but it is not unusual to find such phrases as "ability and willingness to teach students with limited English proficiency is required," or "improving English skills is a critical part of instruction at all levels." Some institutions indicate a preference for fluency in English and "one of the UN languages."

Most international employers clearly indicate the preferred method of receiving applications. For example, the position announcement may specifically instruct you to download application materials from the institution's web site or to fax or e-mail your CV. In the absence of specific directions, you can use the conventional method of submitting your materials via air mail. Initial contacts by fax or e-mail are appropriate and preferred. Supplemental materials can be submitted under separate cover if requested.

If you have created a web site that contains your CV and other professional materials be sure to inform the employer about its existence and its location. This can save both you and the employer a great deal of time and should enhance your candidacy.

Conference Version

Professional conferences frequently provide some type of employment assistance. A job seeker can submit a CV to be reviewed by administrators seeking faculty or staff for available or anticipated positions. Some organizations will accept your CV even if you are not in attendance at the conference.

Pay particular attention to conference guidelines for CV submission. Placement services at professional meetings routinely limit the number of pages permitted. Regardless of how many pages you think you need, follow directions and scale your CV down to size. Pages that exceed the limit are often simply discarded.

Conferences often afford the opportunity to discuss employment possibilities with representatives from colleges and universities. Formal interviews can be scheduled in advance, others are arranged on the spot. Informal conversations at receptions, on the conference floor, or following breakout sessions can develop into serious discussions of employment possibilities.

Take extra copies of your CV to distribute as the opportunity arises. As a job seeker, use your CV as your business card. Don't be hesitant about offering it to people you encounter at professional meetings. It is a good idea to follow up on these contacts by sending a copy of your CV with a short letter after you leave the conference.

Condensed Version

A brief overview of your professional career can be prepared for those occasions when you need to provide basic information without much detail. For example, when you are invited to address a professional meeting or to present a workshop, your condensed CV will be welcomed by the person responsible for introducing you to the group. Your condensed CV not only makes your presenter's task easier, it helps to assure that the information you consider most relevant is conveyed.

International CV

Strategic Features

- Languages and Travel category appears on first page to emphasize multi-language ability and related international experience

- Publications moved to second page, allowing all Teaching and Related Experiences annotations to appear together on page one (compare modifications with document prepared for stateside job search, pages 42–43)

- Data relevant for international considerations, not regularly a part of a CV in the United States, has been placed at the end of the document

~

Take a careful look at this sample if

- you are interested in preparing or modifying an existing CV for international teaching or research positions

ALEXIA SAMPRAS

121 Academic Hall   Any City, State 12345   U.S.A.
(101) 555-1111   a-sampras@usb.edu

ACADEMIC BACKGROUND:

Ph.D. Curriculum and Instruction Emphasis: Developmental Reading
University of Santa Barbara, Santa Barbara, California. Anticipated May 2000
Dissertation title: *Developmentally Appropriate Learning Styles for the Student with Second Language Acquisition.* K. T. Russ, Ph.D. Adviser
Comprehensive areas: Elementary Education, Developmental Reading, English as a Second Language

M.A. Elementary Education - Bilingual Emphasis, 1995
Lewis and Clark University, Portland Oregon
Thesis: *Early Reading Patterns of Immigrant Children.*, B.E. Fine, Ph.D. Adviser

B.A. Spanish and Elementary Education, 1990
University of Hawaii at Manoa   *cum laude   Phi Beta Kappa*

RESEARCH INTERESTS:

Emergent Literacy	Children's Literature	Ethnography
Integrated Language Arts	English as a Second Language	Infant Cognition

INTERNATIONAL FELLOWSHIP:

Newman Graduate Fellowship for International Research & Fieldwork, Fall 1998
Collected data and conducted extensive fieldwork regarding early reading programs in central China. Presented seminars, worked with community teams to establish learning centers in rural areas, and collaborated with Nanjing Normal University faculty to develop curricula for practicing teachers.

LANGUAGES AND TRAVEL:

Fluent in Spanish and Mandarin; Shanghai resident, (8 years)
Advanced Spanish language studies, Mexico City and Madrid Institute, (4 summers)
Rotary Foreign Exchange Student Scholarship, Madrid, Spain, (1 year)

GRADUATE APPOINTMENTS:

Research Assistant, Curriculum and Instruction, UC-Santa Barbara, 1999-present
Research, collect, and analyze data for a federally funded project on implications of technology and literacy in southern provinces of China. Work collaboratively with College of Education faculty, State Department, and Minister of Education-Shanghai.

Teaching Assistant, College of Education, UC-Santa Barbara, 1998-199
Complete responsibility for two sections of Bilingual Methods for Elementary Teachers. Worked closely with students in understanding language acquisition and implementing effective classroom teaching strategies.

TEACHING AND RELATED EXPERIENCES:

Supervisor - Student Teachers, Lewis and Clark University, 1994-1995
Observed student teachers, provided feedback and support, and conducted formal three-way conferences among student teacher, college supervisor and cooperating teacher. Organized a regular seminar, evaluated student progress, and assigned grades.

Classroom Teacher, International School of Shanghai, 1992-1994
Prekindergarten teacher (ages 4 to 5). Collaborative setting stressing developmentally appropriate approaches to learning. Worked closely with faculty and student interns from Shanghai International University.

Classroom Teacher, Department of Education, Honolulu, Hawaii, 1990-1992
Bilingual first grade teacher and member of the mentor program.

PUBLICATIONS:

Sampras, A. (1999). <u>Preschool readiness and intercultural expectations</u>. Manuscript submitted for publication.

Sampras, A. (in press). Learning styles and missing the grade. <u>Teacher Magazine</u>.

Sampras, A., Alot, R., & Fine, B.E. (1999). Cognitive abilities and reading strategies of four year olds. <u>Journal of Early Childhood</u>. <u>36</u>, 153-157.

Sampras, A. (1998). Recognizing appropriate learning styles of preschoolers. <u>Journal of Early Childhood</u>. <u>33</u>, 149-151.

Sampras, A., & Goode, B. (1997, October). Developmentally appropriate language arts for preschoolers. <u>Preschool Times</u>, pp. 53-57.

SERVICE:

Memberships:
National Association for the Education of Young Children
Association for Childhood Education International
International Reading Association
National Council of Teachers of English

Leadership:
Executive Officer (1999- present), Pi Lambda Theta
Chair, Region 10 Education Early Childhood Advisory Council, 1999
Board Member, Idaho Council on Bilingual Education, 1996-1998
President, Pacific Council on Head Start, 1996
Representative, Education Committee, Region 10 Informational Sciences Board, 1996

Consulting:
Bilingual Learning Centers, Inc., Washington D.C.
The Infant Centers, Boise, Idaho; Omaha, Nebraska; Santa Clara, California
University Center for Child Development, Idaho State University
Aerospace Childcare Center, Seattle, Washington

Presentations
"Bilingual Training: Successful Strategies," invited address at Washington State Bilingual Conference, Seattle, May, 1999
"Parent Collaboration in Bilingual Settings," guest speaker, Oakland City Schools Consortium, Oakland, December, 1998
"Technology and Second Language Acquisition," panel member, State Conference on Educational Technology, Los Angeles, March, 1997

RELEVANT DATA

Citizenship: United States
One dependent, age 10; partner (Master's Degree-Music, 10 years experience teaching)

DOSSIER:

Career Development Center, Office of Student Services
Any City, State 12345 Telephone: (101) 555-1000   FAX: (101) 555-1010
Portfolio available for review upon request

Conference CV
Strategic Features

- Conference version trimmed to two pages to meet "conference/convention requirements." Categories have been condensed to include major ideas or responsibilities of positions

- Categories such as Teaching, Research, and Activities and Awards have been combined and renamed to save space

- "Selected Presentations" implies that additional materials exist

~

Take a careful look at this sample if

- you need to condense your CV to fit the prescribed limits of a professional association or service agency

J. JOE BISHOP

21 University Avenue   Any City, State 12345   joe@uiowa.edu   101.555.1000

DEGREES

Ph.D. Candidate: Social Studies Education, The University of Iowa, Iowa City, 1995-present
Dissertation Topic: Conceptions of Democracy and Civic Education in the Czech Republic
Comprehensive Areas: International/ Comparative Education, Language/Culture, Sociology of Culture
M.A. Anthropology, The University of Iowa, 1995
Paper: The Social Context of Representations: An Investigation into the Commentary on the
    Mead-Freeman Controversy.
Post-Masters Study, Rhetoric and Communication, University of Oregon, Eugene, 1989-1990
M.A. Sociology, The University of Iowa, 1989
Thesis: Self Referential Behavior in North American Protestant Christianity.
B.A. *cum laude*, Winona State University, Winona, Minnesota, 1987
Majors: Communication Theory & Psychology   Minors: Sociology & Mathematics
A.A. *with honors*, Rainy River Community College, International Falls, Minnesota, 1984

RESEARCH AND TEACHING INTERESTS

Research: International and comparative education; social and historical cognition; natural language
analysis of academic, educational, religious, and popular culture artifacts and behaviors.
Teaching: Educational anthropology; human relations; educational sociology; comparative and
international education; introductory sociology and anthropology; language and culture; knowledge,
religion, and popular culture; research methods; social and cultural theory; pedagogy.

SPECIAL TRAINING

Languages: Oral skills: French (fair); Spanish (fair); Czech (basic); Russian (basic); Mongolian (basic)
Reading skills: French (good); Spanish (good); Czech (fair); Russian (basic); Mongolian (functional)
Technology: Webmaster of social studies site (www.uiowa.edu/studies); literate in cross platform software
applications; extensive knowledge of specialized software; Internet and WWW resources

FIELD RESEARCH AND INTERNATIONAL EXPERIENCE:

Dissertation fieldwork, August-October 1997, Czech Republic
Civic Education for Czech Republic Project, May 1997, Prague; January 1997- Amsterdam & Prague
French Canadian cultural orientation, June 1992, Québec, Canada

RESEARCH FUNDING OBTAINED

May 1997: T. Anne Cleary International Dissertation Research Award ($800); Dissertation Research
April 1997: Intensive Russian & Czech program & Stanley Foundation ($250): Czech Language Study
March 1993: Office of Academic Affairs ($500): Mongolian language and culture studies
February 1993: Graduate College ($1000): Mongolian language and culture studies
May 1992: Department of Anthropology ($250): Exploratory research in Québec

WORKS SUBMITTED

Bishop, J. Joe, Historical Understanding Among Pre-Service Social Studies Educators: An Examination
    of the Relationship Between Cognitive Structure and Linguistic Patterns.

Bishop, J. Joe, The Social Context of the Mead-Freeman Controversy

WORKS IN PROGRESS

Bishop, J. Joe, Conceptions of Civic Education and Democracy in the Czech Republic: An Examination
    of the Relationship Between Social Position and Cognitive Structure.

WORKING PAPERS
> Bishop, J. Joe, Stephen G. Wieting and Anastasia Vogt Yuan. "*Ex ungue leonem*: The Social Context of Honorific Addresses -The Case of the ASA Presidential Speeches."
> Bishop, J. Joe, Autopoetic Knowledge Claims Among Protestant Christians: Toward a Theory of Social Complicity.
> Bishop, J. Joe, Project INQUIRT: INQUIRy Training for Teachers.

RESEARCH AND TEACHING EXPERIENCE
> **Adjunct professor**: Sociology; Anthropology; Communication, Kirkwood Community College, (1990-)
> **College supervisor/Czech project coordinator**: Student Teachers, University of Iowa (1996-1998)
> **Test item developer**: Iowa Tests of Development, University of Iowa (Summer 1997)
> **Research assistant**: Civic Education-Czech Republic project; University of Iowa (1996-1997)
> **Teaching assistant**: Social Studies Methods, College of Education, University of Iowa (1996)
> **Teaching assistant**: Anthropology Department, University of Iowa (1991-1993)
> **Research assistant**: Program for International Development, University of Iowa (Spring 1991)
> **Research assistant**: National Resource Center on Family Based Services, University of Iowa (1990)
> **Graduate teaching fellow**: Rhetoric and Communication, University of Oregon (1989-1990)
> **Teaching/research assistant**: Sociology Department, University of Iowa (1987-1989)

SELECTED PRESENTATIONS:
> Bishop, J. Joe, "Flooded Schools and Environmental Problems in the Czech Republic." First Annual International Day, The University of Iowa, 4 November 1997.
> Bishop, J. Joe, "Promoting Social Science Thinking in the Classroom." Iowa Council for the Social Studies Fall, Conference and Workshops. Waterloo, IA, 21 October 1997.
> Bishop, J. Joe, "The 'Self-concept' and Reflective Inquiry." Letní skoly:Vychova k obcantsví a demokracii, Olomouc, Czech Republic, 27 August 1997.
> Bishop, J. Joe,"Thinking About Democracy: Cognitive Structure and Democratic Action."
> Letní skoly:Vychova k obcantsví a demokracii Czech Republic, 27 August 1997.
> Bishop, J. Joe with Radmila Dostálová, "The Civic Education for the Czech Republic Project and the Didactical Text." Letní skoly:Vychova k obcantsví a demokracii. Czech Republic, August 1997.
> Bishop, J. Joe, "Conceptions of Civic Education in the Czech Republic." Policy, Planning, and Leadership Studies Presentation, College of Education, University of Iowa, 22 April 1997.
> Bishop, J. Joe, "The Language of Scholarly Controversy." Policy, Planning, and Leadership Studies Brownbag Presentation, College of Education, University of Iowa, December 1995.
> Bishop, J. Joe, S. G. Wieting and A. Vogt Yuan, "*Ex ungue leonem*: The Social Context of Production of Sociological Knowledge." Iowa Theory Construction Workshop, University of Iowa, 1995.
> Bishop, J. Joe and S. G. Wieting, "The Presidential Standpoint: An Examination of Self-Conceptions of ASA Presidents as a Component of the Social Context of Production of Culture." Paper presentation, Midwest Sociological Society Meetings, Madison, WI, spring 1995.
> Bishop, J. Joe 1992 "Samoan Realities: Implications for Knowledge." "Methodological Issues in Ethnography" session, Qualitative Analysis Conference, May 1992, Carlton University, Ottawa.

AFFLIATIONS AND AWARDS (Selected list)
> Memberships held in AAA, AERA, NCSS, ASA, ICSS, MSS, CIES, CAE, SSSI, AES
> Nominated for life membership - Lambda Alpha; Dean's List; The National Dean's List
> Transfer Honors Scholarship; Fine Arts Scholarship,Winona State University
> Who's Who in American Junior Colleges; Rainy River Community College Valedictorian

Complete CV, writing and research portfolio, and dossier available upon request.

Conference CV - Science
Strategic Features

- Block layout selected to utilize space because annotations are short and concise

- Degrees are placed first because they are recent

- Honors are listed early in the CV to complement the degree and emphasize the candidate's abilities

∼

Take a careful look at this sample if

- you must restrict the length of your CV, as for a conference version; facts are presented without amplification

WILLIAM BUDD

Home: 16 University Avenue   Office: #5 Academic Hall
              Any City, State 12345   Any City, State 12345
              (101) 555-0101   (101) 555-1111

DEGREES

Ph.D. Physical Chemistry, 1999
Washington University, St. Louis, Missouri
Dissertation: Crystal structures of several intermetallic compounds of gadolinium and dyprosium with manganese and iron. J. Pontifex, adviser.

M.A. Chemistry, 1991
University of Minnesota, Minneapolis, Minnesota

B.A. Chemistry/Physics, 1989
Cornell College, Mt. Vernon, Iowa

HONORS

National Science Foundation Fellow, Washington University
John Upson Fellowship, University of Minnesota
Phi Beta Kappa
Phi Lambda Upsilon, honorary chemistry fraternity

TEACHING INTERESTS

Undergraduate courses in physical and organic chemistry
Graduate courses in physical chemistry

RESEARCH INTERESTS

Determination of molecular structure of biologically important compounds
     using x-ray diffraction
Techniques of neutron diffraction

TEACHING

Teaching Assistant, Washington University, St. Louis, Missouri
General Chemistry, Physical Chemistry, 1996-1999
Instructor, Augsburg College, Minneapolis, Minnesota, 1992-1994

RELATED WORK EXPERIENCE

Industrial Researcher, Monsanto Company, 1995
St. Louis, Missouri
Technical Assistant, 3M Company
St. Paul, Minnesota, 1990 (Summer)

AFFILIATIONS:

Alpha Chi Sigma, professional chemistry fraternity
American Chemical Society

ACADEMIC SERVICE:

Departmental Undergraduate Curriculum Committee, 1998-99
Student Member, Search Committee-Graduate School Dean, 1998

DOSSIER:

Placement Office, Any City, State 12345 (101) 555-1000

Condensed CV
Strategic Features

- A single page contains a capsulized overview of professional accomplishments, activities, and recognition

- Facts are presented without annotations or description and without jargon or technical language

- Entries are both condensed and simplified for readers who may not be conversant with the particular specialization or academic discipline

~

Take a careful look at this sample if

- you need to provide information to a master of ceremonies or host preparing to introduce you to a civic group or other general audience

N. A. Jorgensen

Department of Economics, University of Texas at Austin
(512)471-1010(W) (512)471-0011(FAX) na-jorg@utexas.edu

FORMAL EDUCATION

Ph.D.	University of Arizona, Economics, 1980
M.A.	London School of Economics, 1977
B.A.	Cambridge University, Economics/French, 1975

PROFESSIONAL POSITIONS

1993-present	Professor, Department of Economics, University of Texas at Austin
1996-1998	Monee Chair in Economics, Seattle University
1997-1999	Member, U.S. Securities & Exchange Commission, Washington, D.C.
1996-1999	Center Director, Economics & Urban Development, University of Texas at Austin
1991-1993	Associate Professor, Department of Economics, University of Texas at Austin
1989-1991	Research Associate, The Brookings Institution, Washington, D.C.
1985-1989	Assistant Professor, Department of Economics & Social Research, The University of British Columbia, Vancouver
1981-1984	Intern and Research Scientist, International Monetary Fund, Washington, D.C.
1980-1983	Postdoctoral Fellow, Economics & Social Policy, Georgetown University

RESEARCH INTERESTS

- Urban development in emerging countries
- Political intervention in economic decision-making
- Social issues of economic growth
- Monetary economic leadership

INTERNATIONAL EXPERIENCE

Research conducted in United Kingdom, Canada, East Africa, Southeastern Asia
Invited lecturer/presenter at international conferences in Oxford, Glasgow, Geneva, Paris, Seoul
Consultant to international economic agencies working in Malaysia, Philippines, Indonesia
Project review participant, Borneo, New Guinea, Burma, Philippines

PUBLICATIONS

Author of four books including the forthcoming, *The Emerging Politicization of Urban Economics*.
Nearly 100 articles, reviews, essays, and commentaries published since 1985.

OTHER PROFESSIONAL INVOLVEMENT & ACTIVITIES

Distinguished Member, Cambridge Society of Social Scientists; 1998 Scholar, Oxford University
Principal Investigator, Urban migration and resource allocation, Kuala Lumpur
Member and research contributor, International Development Association-Asia Sector
International Relief Site Inspector, CARE, Inc. and Editorial Board, SRI International-East Asia
Review Team Member, American Institute of Social Policy, Malaysia & Burkina Faso
Board Member, International Co-Operative Alliance, London

Turning Your CV into a Résumé

A CV is the preferred document for conveying information about your qualifications for academic positions with primary responsibilities in teaching or research. In most instances, if you are applying for positions outside the academic setting, it will be to your advantage to transform your CV into a résumé.

Even within the academic world, certain types of positions generally call for a résumé rather than a CV. An example of this might be a position as an academic adviser. Your Ph.D. in American Civilization is certainly not irrelevant, but your specific teaching interests and experiences, and exact details of your scholarly activities, are likely to be of lesser importance than other skills.

A résumé is not a second-class document, nor is it less prestigious than a CV. There's nothing degrading about using a résumé instead of a CV.

Resistance or reluctance to make the transformation sends a clear message to non-academic employers: either you're unable to recognize the differences between academic and non-academic environments or unwilling to adapt to the reality of the situation.

Employers outside the academic environment have different needs and expectations. Job seeking documents must be appropriate to the setting and to the responsibilities of the position.

Whatever academic degrees you hold, if you are seeking a position outside the realm of teaching and research, a résumé can be a better choice than a CV.

Simple adjustments may give your CV a new look. On the other hand, major revisions, even a complete restructuring, may be more helpful than a superficial touch-up.

Select Appropriate Categories

The time and effort you devoted to preparing your CV will make it relatively easy to choose appropriate category headings for your new résumé. Many of the categories selected for your CV are still appropriate; some of the headings will need to be revised or replaced.

The following list includes additional category headings appropriate for a résumé.

Résumé Categories

Objective
Career Objective
Employment Objective
Job Objective
Professional Objective
Position Desired

Employment
Experience
Current Employment
Employment Record
Employment History
Other Work
Part-time Work
Summer Work Experience
Military Experience
Additional Experience
Volunteer Experience

Abilities
Competencies
Special Skills
Strengths
Personal Attributes
Achievements
Accomplishments

Computer Skills
Design Skills
Development Skills
Leadership Skills
Administrative Skills
Organizational Skills
Technical Skills

Activities
Related Activities
Community Activities
Community Service
Civic Activities
Other Activities

Interests
Leisure Activities
Special Talents
Personal Interests
References
References Available Upon Request

Transformation Strategies

As you begin to transform your CV into a résumé, consider these techniques for arriving at the most effective presentation of your material.

Rearranging

Transforming your CV into a résumé may be as easy and uncomplicated as rearranging the information you already have on your CV. Lead with your strengths. Your experience may be a stronger selling point than your specific degree or scholarly achievements. If that is the case, move the education section to a less prominent position—even to the very end of the résumé.

Cutting

Shifting the focus from one area to another can often be accomplished through judicious trimming. Annotations about teaching responsibilities can be an important part of a CV; a simple employment history may be sufficient in a résumé that emphasizes other capabilities or interests.

A CV typically lists all publications; your résumé can be selective, listing only the most recent, most relevant, or most prestigious. If you've presented workshops on technical subjects meaningful only to your peers, consider covering the presentations with a summary statement, such as: "presented papers at two national and five regional scientific conferences, 1992-1995."

Some of the information from a CV is irrelevant on a résumé. It is usually a good idea to eliminate such items as principal teachers, dissertation topic or title, lists of graduate courses, or statements about teaching interests.

Adding

Because the résumé is usually intended for a non-academic audience, it can benefit from the addition of several categories not generally seen on the typical CV. For example, a job objective or information about special skills or volunteer activities help to convey information that the academic community usually considers irrelevant.

Job Objectives

Beginning with a statement of your job objective (a category not seen on the typical CV) is one way to give your résumé focus and direction. As the first entry on your résumé, a targeted job objective, concise and unencumbered by excess verbiage, can make a significant contribution.

Sample Job Objectives

Professional public library position. Special interest in reference, computer applications, and materials selection.

Desire entry-level administrative position in a state social service agency.

Special Skills and Competencies

Another option for capturing the reader's attention is to begin with a statement of relevant skills or competencies.

Special Skills

- Technology and multimedia programs
- Written and oral communication
- Research and analytical capabilities
- Supervision and evaluation
- Motivational and organizational skills

Competencies

- Records Management
- Computer Conversion
- Feasibility Studies
- Information Services
- Software Evaluation

Community Service and Organizations

Information about membership and activities in service organizations can give another dimension to your qualifications. Civic activities and community service, usually omitted as irrelevant to academic pursuits, may be of real interest to other potential employers. Volunteer experiences indicate responsible concern for the community and a willingness to be involved.

A résumé, like a CV, reflects your achievements, goals, and career progression. Constructing a résumé requires the same careful planning, evaluation, and revision, as the most elaborate and expansive CV.

Résumé Samples

The following sample résumés can be helpful guides as you prepare a résumé that meets your specific needs. As with the CV samples presented earlier, notice how strategic features identified for each résumé contribute to the total effect. Here, too, the special features are not necessarily linked to the writer's academic discipline. They suggest methods to highlight the writer's strongest assets and to focus on requisite qualities or background or skills acquired and responsibilities exercised in current or previous experiences.

Use the following samples as guides for preparing a résumé that meets your specific needs.

Modern Language Résumé
Strategic Features

- Compare with CV on page 64. Focus has been shifted from academic background to emphasize competencies and accomplishments

- Academic experiences and degrees are highlighted but listed without annotation

- Non-academic employment and interests are presented to counter the academic image

~

Take a careful look at this sample if

- your objective does not require a particular degree or academic discipline

- the abilities you wish to emphasize are not derived from your formal education

MARGUERITE LAROQUE
16 University Avenue, Any City, State 12345
Home: (101) 555-0101   Office: (101) 555-1010

COMPETENCIES

Writing	Translating	Program Development
Speaking	Research	Supervision

ACCOMPLISHMENTS

- Proficient in four languages - French, Norwegian, Spanish, and English
- Participated in $800,000 federally funded project to implement new language program
- Instructed and evaluated more than 500 students over a three-year period
- Chosen to deliver address for regional professional conference with 1000 participants
- Provided individual consultation and tutoring for individuals needing extended help
- Founded Upper Midwest Climbing Club; generated start-up costs from local businesses

PROFESSIONAL EXPERIENCE

Teaching Assistant, French Department
　　Stanford University, Stanford, California, 1998-2000

Teaching Assistant, Literature Department
　　Michigan State University, East Lansing, Michigan, 1996-1998

EDUCATION

　　Luther College, Decorah, Iowa, B.A., English and French, 1996
　　Michigan State University, East Lansing, Michigan, M.A., English, 1998
　　Stanford University, Stanford, California, Ph.D., French, 1998-present

HONORS

Graduated cum laude	Julian Senior Scholarship
Dean's list, six semesters	Leeman Graduate Fellowship Award

PART-TIME AND SUMMER EMPLOYMENT

Copy page proofreader, College News Daily, Stanford, California, 1999-present
Driver/laborer, County Highway Department, LaCrosse, Wisconsin, summers 1991-95

INTERESTS

Mountain climbing, soccer, classical music, cartography

REFERENCES AVAILABLE UPON REQUEST

Computer Science
Résumé
Strategic Features

- Degrees are listed first to emphasize advanced preparation in the specific career field

- Computer Background section identifies competencies and knowledge in specialized area

- Experience categories accentuate responsibility and skills; annotations use descriptive phrases that are quickly read

~

Take a careful look at this sample if

- you want to emphasize specific strengths and training in a particular area

- your experience includes university teaching assistantships and company-based employment

ALEC SANORES
16 University Ave Any City, State 12345
(101) 555-0009   a-sanores@bu.edu

DEGREES   **M.S.**   **Computer Science**, May 1998
Boston University, Boston, Massachusetts
Thesis: Development of a Digital Circuit Simulator

B.S.   **Math/Computer Science,** June 1995
Stetson University, Deland, Florida
Undergraduate Fulbright Scholar   *summa cum laude*

COMPUTER   *Systems Used:* VAX (Unix), IBM 360/370 (MVS), HP
BACKGROUND   *Languages:*   PL/1, Fortran, Pascal, IBM Assembly, COBOL, C++

Theoretical Background:
Data Structures, Computer Architecture, Operating Systems, Concurrent
Programming, Formal Specification of Programming Languages, Data
Abstraction, Hardware Description Languages, Distributed Databases.

FELLOWSHIP   **Computer Analysis Fellowship**, Market Research Laboratory, University of
Miami and Economic Development Council of Florida. January - May, 1998.
Responsibilities included collecting, processing and analyzing market research data
on MacIntosh and IBM computer software. Prepared summations of the findings
for management meetings and for quarterly reports. Observed planning and
development meetings for market research and small business concerns.

TEACHING   **Instructor**, COBOL, University of Tennessee, spring 1999
EXPERIENCE   **Programming Instructor**, Saturday & Evening course - level I, fall 1998
Teaching Assistant, Computer Science Department, Boston University, fall 1997

Responsibilities in above positions included lecturing for two classes six
times per week, designing of tests and programs, and assigning grades.
Supervised graduate level students who acted as graders. Complete
responsibility for all aspects of Fortran and COBOL courses.

BUSINESS   **Network Specialist**, College of Business, University of Tennessee, May, 1998
EXPERIENCE   Responsibilities include maintaining and upgrading electronic communication
and access to information via the college network. Train professional and
support staff in network usage to insure access and protect confidential records.
(50% appointment)

Computer Programmer, Tech, Inc., Nashville, Tennessee, July 1995 - July 1996
Responsibilities included data analysis, database programming and the designing
of computer programs for performing artists located in the Nashville area.

References Provided Upon Request

Library Résumé
Strategic Features

- Areas of knowledge, followed by course highlights, immediately identify strengths and interests; useful alternative to Job Objective category

- To eliminate repetition, responsibilities of three positions are summarized

- Reference category does not list a placement office; writer offers to provide references

Take a careful look at this sample if

- you have held a number of positions with similar responsibilities

- your specific skills are not reflected in previous academic or employment experiences

J. EDWARD AUSTEN

ADDRESS

16 University Avenue
Any City, State 12345
(101) 555-0009

AREAS OF KNOWLEDGE

Computer Languages:
COBOL, FORTRAN, C++
Hardware & Software Evaluation

Records Maintenance
Information Services
Feasibility Studies

COURSE HIGHLIGHTS

• Programming Language Concepts
• Computer Packages for
   Statistical Analysis
• Database Management Systems

• Systems Software Design
• Principles of Management
• Management of Libraries

EXPERIENCE

Graduate Practicum Student, Fall, 2000
Tuscaloosa Public Library , Tuscaloosa, Alabama
Graduate Internship, Spring, 2000
West Side Branch, Tuscaloosa County Libraries, Tuscaloosa, Alabama
Circulation Clerk, 1996-99
Livingston University Library, Livingston, Alabama
   Responsibilities in these positions included:
   computer applications
   program planning and publicity
   budget preparation
   outreach programming and public services
   evaluation and maintenance studies

COMMUNITY ACTIVITIES

Volunteer Librarian, Tuscaloosa Community Center
Member, Tuscaloosa County Oral History Society
Volunteer, Children's Hands-On Museum (CHOM)
Fundraising Committee, Cultural Olympiad/Southern Arts Federation

EDUCATION

Masters Degree in Library and Information Studies, 2000
   University of Alabama, Tuscaloosa, Alabama

Bachelor of Arts Degree, with honors, in German and Sociology, 1998
   Livingston University, Livingston, Alabama

HONORS & AWARDS

Scholarship,University of Alabama - Library and Information Studies
Dean's list, 1997-98, Livingston University
State of Alabama Tuition Scholarship
Phi Theta Kappa honorary society

REFERENCES

Upon request

Law Résumé
Strategic Features

- Layout allows for complete use of the page providing maximum space for relevant degree, assistantship, and employment data

- Résumé material was tailored for a one-page version focusing on "law related activities and accomplishments" (compare with two-page CV on pages 69–70)

- To conserve space, responsibilities of three assistantships were combined in one annotation

- Résumé is careful to highlight items desired by law recruiters, e.g., class rank and GPA

~

Take a careful look at this sample if

- you are applying for non-academic positions that prefer a one-page résumé

JAMES J. HUBERTY
21 University Ave, Any City, State 12345
jj@uiowa.edu   101.555.1010

DEGREES: THE UNIVERSITY OF IOWA, IOWA CITY, IOWA
Juris Doctor and Master in Business Administration, May 1998
Honors: College of Law Scholar Tuition Scholarship; School of Management Fellowship
Activities: Honor and Ethics Code Committee Member; Student Marketing Association Member
Class Rank: Top 15%   GPA: JD-80.5/90   MBA-3.83/4.00

Bachelor of Science Degree in Business Administration, May 1991; Majors: Finance, Marketing
Graduated *with distinction*   Dean's List
University Honors Scholarship   University Tuition Scholarship
Maytag Corporation Scholarship   Melville Corporation Scholarship

LAW INTERNSHIP
Summer Associate, Lord, Bissell & Brook, Chicago, Illinois, May 1997 - August 1997
Worked as an intern in Lord, Bissell & Brook, a firm of 99 partners and 135 associates specializing in insurance, litigation, and corporate law.
Specific intern responsibilities included:
- Extensive research performed regarding a variety of legal issues.
- Drafted legal memoranda for internal and external use.
- Named a contributing author to client newsletter.
- Worked closely with firm members in several different departments.

GRADUATE ASSISTANTSHIPS: THE UNIVERSITY OF IOWA
Teaching Assistant Supervisor-Introduction to Law, College of Business Administration, 8/96 - 5/98
Teaching Assistant-Introduction to Law, College of Business Administration, 8/95 - 5/98
Legal Research Assistant, College of Law, Summer 1995
Responsibilities for above positions included:
- Coordinated and directed four graduate-level teaching assistants in *Introduction to Law* course.
- Materials focused on defining legal rules and principles, and illuminating their rationale.
- Designed database to manage administrative tasks including grading, enrollment and attendance.
- Researched case law and academic journals regarding civil forfeiture and its legality considering the implications of the Double Jeopardy Clause.

PROFESSIONAL EMPLOYMENT
Investment Analyst, Old Republic Asset Management Corporation, Chicago, Illinois, 4/92 - 8/94
Assisted Corporate Investment Officer/Portfolio Manager in management of approximately $2.5 billion asset portfolio. Evaluated investment opportunities and provided reports regarding the status and makeup of the investment portfolios under management; conducted extensive communication and trading activity and institutional brokerage services; created and maintained portfolio database reports to be utilized for corporate and strategic management purposes. Passed first of three examinations for CPA. Specific responsibilities: cash management, securities transactions, investment research, analysis.

RELATED ACTIVITIES
Writing Center Tutor, University of Law School, 1996 - 1998
Volunteer leadership positions, Student Marketing Association, 1996 - 1998

References and writing sample available upon request.

Instructional Design and Technology Résumé

Strategic Features

- Document omits all graphics, italics, and bold features for submission to organizations that use scanning technology to screen and store resumes.

- Degrees are listed first because academic training is current and terminal degree is required for desired position

- Special Skills category clearly identifies specific proficiencies and areas of expertise

- Consulting and teaching categories contain concise annotations of directly related responsibilities; these categories could be reversed for academic or professional situations

~

Take a careful look at this sample if

- your professional experiences can be divided into distinct categories

- you have substantial related experience prior to completing your advanced degree

JAMIE SMITHE

16 University Avenue   Any City, State   12345   (101) 555-0101
jsmithe@ugeorgia.edu   www.design/is.htm

DEGREES

Ph.D.   INSTRUCTIONAL DESIGN & TECHNOLOGY
             University of Georgia, Athens, Georgia, 1997 - present

M.A.   COMPUTER SCIENCE   Iowa State University, Ames, Iowa, 1994 - 1996

B.A.   HISTORY with honors   Grinnell College, Grinnell, Iowa, 1992

SPECIAL SKILLS

Computer Programming   Project Design & Development   Client Consultation
Project Supervision   Multimedia Production   Needs Assessment

TECHNOLOGICAL EXPERTISE

C++, HTML, CGI scripting, and JavaScript. Built Web sites for two classes: Multimedia
and Global Networks. View at www.educ.esl.w101 and www.educ.mm/coe5.htm
Multimedia skills: photo and authoring software, video/audio digitizing, CD-ROM Mastering

CONSULTING EXPERIENCE

Training Consultant, Zmok Promotions, Inc., Atlanta, Georgia, Fall 1998.
Hired to conceptualize and build a series of Web sites for educational programs. Responsibilities
involve regular client consultations, budget management, and technical assistant supervision.

Training Consultant, East Designs, Inc., Atlanta, Georgia, Spring 1998.
Designed a multilingual computer-based training program for factory line workers. Experience
included consulting with team management, conducting research, interviewing and hiring
translators, computer programming, and pilot testing.

TEACHING EXPERIENCE

Webmaster and Teaching Assistant, College of Education, University of Georgia, 1998 - present
Responsible for redesigning and maintenance of the college-wide Web site; taught HTML and
Web design to faculty and students. Implementing and evaluating a two semester hour
multi-media course offered to graduate and undergraduate students.

Graduate Teaching Assistant, Multimedia Production Lab, University of Georgia, 1997
Responsible for instruction and production of specialized programs in the College of Nursing.
Collaborated with faculty, clinical staff and practitioners in developing programs for classroom
and commercial use. Developed interactive Web course for two distance learning classes.

Peace Corps Volunteer, Kingston, Jamaica, 1992-1994
Developed and presented workshops to rural educators. Created special instructional resources
and established on-going reading programs to ensure continued use of library resources.

PROFESSIONAL AFFILIATIONS

National Society for Performance and Instruction
Association for Educational Communication and Technology

Web Portfolio and References Available Upon Request

Student Personnel Résumé

Strategic Features

- Essential information about academic background and relevant experience is presented on the first page

- Subsequent page provides overview of professional and community activities

- Skills not represented elsewhere are identified in Special Interests category

∼

Take a careful look at this sample if

- your only relevant experience has been acquired as part of your degree program

- you need to provide detailed annotations; using the full width of the page conserves space and makes information easily accessible

LEE S. ABBOTT

16 University Avenue • Any City, State 12345 • (101) 555-0009
l-abbott@ui.edu • www.leeabbott.htm

ACADEMIC BACKGROUND

M.A.   Student Personnel and Counselor Education, June 1998 - present
Indiana University, Bloomington, Indiana

B.S.   Computer Science/Psychology, May 1997 *with Distinction*
Notre Dame University, Notre Dame, Indiana

RELATED PROFESSIONAL EXPERIENCE

Graduate Assistantships:

Academic Advisor, Undergraduate Advisory Office, Indiana University, Fall 1999- present
Advised lower division students and unassigned special non-degree students; interviewed
students on academic probation, and organized advance CLEP registration.

Teaching Assistant, Introductory Psychology, Indiana University Extension System, Summer 1998.
Responsible for instruction and grade assignment for two discussion sections; included designing
and grading quizzes, answering student questions and keeping office hours.

Practica:

Career Development Office, Indiana University, Fall, 1998. Assisted in the day-to-day operations
of a comprehensive placement center. Advised seniors about resume writing techniques and
interview awareness, job-seeking software, and employer databases. Participated in classroom
presentations, placement office orientation seminars, and Career Fair organizational sessions.

Special Support Services, Spring Component, Indiana University, Spring, 1998. Worked with
staff on special projects, met with prospective minority and educationally disadvantaged
students, and coordinated the Multicultural Project-1998 with the Eastside YWCA.

Orientation Services, Indiana University - Calumet Campus, Summer, 1998. Assisted director with
summer freshman orientation programs, and with special projects related to transfer students.

EMPLOYMENT

Computer Programmer, Comsat Laboratories, Clarksburg, Maryland, May 1997 - August 1998
Member of the satellite telecommunications research and development team. One-year
assignment focused on subsystems and technologies testing; data analysis and report writing.

WORKSHOPS AND CONVENTIONS

Poster Session, "Technology and Student Services," American Counseling Association Convention, San Diego, California, April, 1999.

Workshop Leader, "Advising the New Student," State Student Services Conference, South Bend, Indiana, March, 1999.

Discussion Facilitator, "Multicultural Issues in Counseling," Regional Conference on Counseling, Lexington, Kentucky, October, 1998.

Attended the ACA Convention, Indianapolis, Indiana, March, 1998.

MEMBERSHIPS

Professional:

Indiana Consortium for Minority Students   American College Personnel Association
Association for Multicultural Counseling   American Counseling Association
    and Development

Campus:

Graduate Student Development Association - Indiana University
    President, 1998 - 1999   Member, 1997 - present

SPECIAL INTERESTS

Computer Programming   Spanish Language and Culture
    (C++, FORTRAN, COBOL, BASIC)   Public Relations
Adaptive Technologies   Organizational Behavior

VOLUNTEER EXPERIENCE

Part-time counselor and small-group leader, The Half-Way House, Bloomington, 1999-present
Assistant and patient advocate, Free Medical Clinic, Bloomington, 1998-1999
Patient information assistant and interpreter, Southern County Emergency Center, 1997-1998
Big Brother Pals Association, South Bend Chapter, South Bend, Indiana, 1995-1997

ACADEMIC HONORS

Dean's List; President's Citation   National Merit Scholarship Recipient
J. Hunter Academic Scholarship   Psi Chi (undergraduate honorary in psychology)

Credentials: Office of Student Services, Any City, State   12345 (101) 555-1000

Athletic Administration
Strategic Features

- Job objective, rarely used in a CV or academic résumé, pinpoints exact type of position sought

- Areas of Expertise and Career Overview categories are listed early to demonstrate progressive responsibilities and qualifications

- Career Highlights combine coaching success, leadership, and personal achievement

~

Take a careful look at this sample if

- a summary of your professional experiences and achievements will have greater impact than a comprehensive list

I. M. WELLMAN
16 University Avenue, Any City, State 12345
(101) 555-0101 (h) (101) 555-1010 (w)

Objective	Collegiate Athletic Administration

Areas of Expertise	Budget management/fund raising Marketing/promotions Selection and management of personnel Facilitating recruitment and retention of athletes Communicate clearly and effectively with campus administration

Career Overview	Assistant Athletic Administrator 2 years Head Coach 3 years High School Teacher/Coach 2 years

Education	Ph.D.	Athletic Administration, 1998 - (in progress) University of California-Davis
	M.A.	Leisure Studies, 1993 University of Michigan, Ann Arbor
	B.S.	Physical Education and Biology, 1991 University of Texas at Austin

Career Highlights	• Appointed to President's Council on Physical Fitness, 1998 • Elected to West Coast Athletic Advisory Board, 1998 • Selected Outstanding Coach, Southeastern Conference, 1996 • Chosen Eastern College Coach-of-the-Year, 1995 • Coached Michigan State High School Championship 3A Girl's Basketball Team • Named to Kodak All-American Team; Olympic Tryouts; Selected Conference Player-of-the-Year, 1990

Current Experience	Assistant Director of Athletics, July 1998 - present Santa Rosa Junior College, Santa Rosa, California Assist with planning, directing and reviewing the institutional programs and sports activities and operations of the Santa Rosa athletic, intramural, community recreation and fitness programs. Facilitate the recruitment and retention of student athletes and manage fund-raising and promotion efforts for athletic programs.

I.M. Wellman
Page 2

**Coaching
Experience**

Head Basketball Coach, 1995 - 1998
Tennessee State University, Nashville, Tennessee
Record: 81-19   Conference Champions: 1996, 1997
Qualified for National Basketball Tournament

Volunteer Assistant Coach, 1994 -1995
East Texas State University, Commerce, Texas
Worked under the tuteledge of Coach B.J. Henes

Head Girl's Basketball Coach, 1991 - 1994
South High School, Battle Creek, Michigan
Class 3A State Champions: 1993

**Professional
Activities**

Faculty Council Representative
Chair, Alumni Sports Foundation Fund
Advisor, Student Athletic Advisory Committee
Member, American Alliance for Health, Physical Education,
   Recreation & Dance (AAHPERD)
Executive Council, AAHPERD
Member, American Association of University

**College
Achievements**

Academic All-American
Kodak All-American Player
Captain, University of Texas Basketball Team
First Team All-Conference, two years
M.V.P. Selection - Southwest Conference

**Community
Service**

Chair, Special Olympics State Committee
Spokesperson, Youth Activities Council of California
Member, Board of Directors, United Action for Youth
Volunteer, Santa Rosa Habitat for Humanity
Volunteer, Big Brother/Big Sister, Inc.
State Advisory Board, High School Athletics Council

References Available Upon Request

Cover Letters

The term "cover letter" is perhaps unfortunate because it tends to minimize the effect of introductory correspondence. The function of a cover letter is not simply to present your CV. An effective letter can be a valuable marketing tool. Along with your CV, it serves to:
- introduce you,
- represent you to good advantage, and
- stimulate interest in your background and qualifications.

Creativity is an asset, but don't waste time worrying about innovative approaches or attention-getting devices. Imagine yourself speaking directly to the reader; let the tone and vocabulary of your letter represent your conversation at its best.

In the early stages of a job search, a cover letter may be sent to inquire about potential openings. Even if a position has not been advertised, you may send a letter and a copy of your CV to selected institutions. A letter of inquiry can help you to discover opportunities in preferred locations or in the type of college or university of greatest interest to you.

When a position has been advertised, a letter of application, along with a copy of your CV, is your entry into the pool of applicants to be considered as candidates for the position. Use the letter to match your strengths to the description of the announced vacancy.

This is no time to be humble. Describe your achievements confidently, but allow them to speak for themselves—don't negate or inflate them with stilted prose or pompous diction.

A good cover letter can be a powerful means of expressing your genuine interest in the available position, highlighting your qualifications, and promoting your candidacy.

The cover letter can be used as a screening device. Along with the CV, it may be circulated to each member of the search committee. Some committees will expect to read every document submitted by each applicant. In other situations, members of the search committee are provided only with copies of the CV; the cover letter may be seen only by the head of the committee or another designated person.

It's almost impossible to predict the exact role of your cover letter in the selection process. Whether your letter receives cursory attention from a single individual or careful scrutiny by an entire search committee, it will have an impact. A thoughtful, intelligent, convincing letter could be a deciding factor.

Be sure that your letter will pass initial inspection and create a good first impression. All that is required is to be correct—no errors, no shortcuts, no idiosyncracies.

Salutation

Whenever possible, send your letter to a specific person. If you do not have the name of an individual or if the advertisement directs you to write to a department, use the simplified style of business letter which omits both the salutation and the complimentary closing.

Be cautious about salutations—some are dated, trite, and inappropriate. A number of them could be considered offensive. Take no risks.

Avoid These Dead-end Dears

Dear Chair	Dear People
Dear Chairman	Dear Person
Dear Chairperson	Dear Reader
Dear Colleague	Dear Search Committee
Dear Dean	Dear Sir
Dear Department Head	Friends and Colleagues
Dear Director	Gentlemen
Dear Faculty Member	Good Morning
Dear Friends	Hello
Dear Gentlepeople	Ladies
Dear Head	Mesdames
Dear Ladies	Sirs
Dear Ma'am	To Whom it May Concern
Dear Madam	

Letter-Writing Tips

- Use a letter-quality printer to produce original letters; photocopies or form letters are not acceptable.
- Choose stationery that matches or coordinates with your CV.
- Select a conventional, easily legible font or typeface.
- Adopt a standard business-letter format. See samples following this section.
- Whenever possible, write to a specific person, using the exact name and title provided.
- Use the simplified style of business letter (no salutation, no complimentary closing) if you are unable to determine the name of an individual to whom your letter should be sent.
- Begin with a statement of purpose; refer to the position by title.
- It is a courtesy to tell how you learned of the vacancy (such as a professional journal, newspaper, departmental notice).

And more tips:

- Refer to pertinent information about the institution or the department.
- Emphasize preparation and experience related to the stated responsibilities of the position.
- Be concise, but be thorough. It is permissible to use a page and a half or even two pages, but anything more is probably excessive.
- Indicate compliance with requests for materials or supporting documents (transcripts, references, dossier, writing samples).
- Proofread to eliminate any errors of grammar, spelling, or fact.
- Keep a copy for your records. You will need it for any subsequent communication with the employer.

Sample Cover Letters

The following letters should help you get started. Use them as guides for content and models for appropriate business letter styles.

Sample Letter of Application

21 College Street
Any City, State 12345
March 28, 1999

Search Committee
Department of English
University of Oregon
Campus Box 449
Eugene, Oregon 97403

Please consider me as an applicant for the assistant professorship in the Department of English at the University of Oregon which was announced in the March Job List of the Modern Language Association. Currently, I am a candidate for a Ph.D. in English at Michigan State University. My dissertation, "Aesthetic Distance in the Early Comedies of Ben Johnson," focuses on Johnson's use of comic distortion and fable to achieve aesthetic distance. Research for the dissertation was begun with Professor Abe Scholl during my year at Oxford University as a R.B. Cann Literary Fellow. My dissertation advisor at Michigan State University is Professor K. Johs-Kerus.

I chose to include expository writing as one area of my comprehensive exams because I am genuinely interested in the teaching of writing. My experiences, which are highlighted on the enclosed CV, include both teaching and research in this area. As a teaching assistant in the Communications Program at Michigan State University, I was responsible for all aspects of a required freshman course, including instruction and grading as well as individual conferences and student advising. During the current year my responsibilities encompass compilation of an annotated bibliography and review of the literature pertaining to methods of teaching expository writing as a part of a federal grant administered by Professors Johs-Kerus and C. Struttgard.

My complete dossier, including the three letters of recommendation requested in the advertisement, is being forwarded to you from the Placement Center at Michigan State University. If there are additional application materials to be completed or if writing samples are desired, please contact me. If interested, writing samples, a dissertation abstract, and descriptions of courses taught and performance evaluations can be viewed on my Web-based portfolio at: www.jones/portfolio.htm.

I would welcome the opportunity to discuss this position with you in person and can make arrangements for an interview at your convenience.

(signature)

Terry Jones

Enclosure

NOTE: The letter style is a simplified business letter format. Use this style when names of contact people have not been included in the advertisement. This style eliminates both the salutation and the complimentary closing.

Sample Letter of Inquiry

#5 Academic Hall
Any City, State 12345
March 24, 1999

V. J. DeSaint, Ph.D.
Chair, Search Committee
English Department
Kenyon College
P.O. Box 24567S
Gambier, Ohio 43022

Dear Professor DeSaint:

The purpose of this letter is to inquire if vacancies are anticipated in the English Department at Kenyon College for which I might be considered. My course work for the Ph.D. has been completed at Michigan State University and I am currently in the final stages of my dissertation.

I am genuinely interested in the teaching of writing and I chose to include expository writing as one area of my comprehensive exams. My master's program at Yale University and my doctoral studies have provided a broad and rich background in literature. I am qualified and interested in teaching survey courses in both British and American literature and upper-division courses in British literature from the Renaissance through the Victorian era.

As you will note from the enclosed CV, my teaching experience has concentrated on the development of speaking and writing skills. As a teaching assistant in the communications program at Michigan State University, I was responsible for all aspects of a required freshman course, including instruction and grading as well as individual conferences and student advising. Last year I was selected to serve as a research assistant with Professors K. Johs-Kerus and Carla Struttgard in the implementation of a federally funded grant to introduce a new undergraduate program in expository writing.

As a graduate of Bowdoin College, I have particular interest in working with under-graduates in a small liberal arts environment. If teaching openings are anticipated, I could easily arrange to visit with you at the national conference or at a time and place convenient to you. A self-addressed stamped envelope is enclosed if application materials are available. If interested, writing samples, a dissertation abstract, and descriptions of courses taught can be viewed on my Web-based portfolio at: www.jones/portfolio.htm. My dossier and supporting documents will be sent upon request.

Sincerely yours,

(signature)
Terry Jones

Enclosures

Appendix I
Professional Associations

Professional associations offer a variety of publications including journals, newsletters, research reports, conference proceedings, yearbooks, membership directories, and job bulletins. Some organizations offer direct assistance to job seekers and employers at regional and national conferences. Contact the appropriate association for complete information about memberships, publications, and services.

In the following sections, association names, addresses, phone numbers, and web site URL's (if available) are listed. Although many professional associations maintain permanent headquarters, some associations relocate with changes in leadership.

Arts and Communication

Arts & CommunicationAmerican Arts Alliance
1319 F Street NW, Suite 500
Washington, D.C. 20004
(202)737-1727
http://www.tmn.com/Artswire/www/aaa/aaahome.html

American Choral Directors Association
Box 6310
Lawton, Oklahoma 73506
(405)355-8161
http://www.ithaca.edu/admin/cca2/acda.htm

American Council for the Arts
1 East 53rd Street
New York, New York 10022-4201
(202)223-2787
http://www.artsusa.org/

American Musicological Society
201 S. 34th Street
Philadelphia, Pennsylvania 19104-6313
(215)898-9698
http://musdra.ucdavis.edu/documents/AMS/AMS.html

American Society for Theatre Research
Box 1897
Department of Theatre, Speech and Dance
Brown University
Providence, Rhode Island 02912
(401)863-3289
http://www.music.uiuc.edu/theatre/astr

American String Teachers Association
1806 Robert Futon Drive, Suite 300
Reston, Virginia 22091
(703)476-1317
http://www.astaweb.com/

Association for Education in Journalism and Mass Communication
College of Journalism
University of South Carolina
1621 College Street
Columbia, South Carolina 29208-0251
(803)777-2005
http://www.aejmc.sc.edu/online/home.html

Association for Educational Communications and Technology
1025 Vermont Avenue NW, Suite 820
Washington, D.C. 20005
(202)347-7834
http://www.aect.org

Association of Teachers of Technical Writing
Department of Rhetoric
University of Minnesota
64 Classroom Office Building
1994 Buford Avenue
St. Paul, Minnesota 55108-6122
http://english.ttu/ATTW/

Broadcast Education Association
1771 N Street NW
Washington, D.C. 20036
(202)429-5354
http://www.usu.edu/~bea/

College Art Association
275 7th Avenue
New York, New York 10001
http://www.collegeart.org/

College Music Society
202 W. Spruce Street
Missoula, Montana 59802-4202
(406)721-9616
http://www.music.org/

Congress on Research in Dance
c/o Dance Department
State University of New York
Brockport, New York 14420
(716)395-2590

Educational Theatre Association
3368 Central Parkway
Cincinnati, Ohio 45225
(513)559-1996
http://www.etassoc.org/

Music Educators National Conference
1806 Robert Fulton Drive
Reston, Virginia 20191-4348
(703)860-4000
http://www.menc.org/

Music Teachers National Association
The Carew Tower
441 Vine Street, Suite 505
Cincinnati, Ohio 45202-2814
(513)421-1420
http://www.mtna.com/

National Art Education Association
1916 Association Drive
Reston, Virginia 22091-1590
(703)860-8000
http://www.naea-reston.org/

National Association of Teachers of Singing
JU Station
2800 University Boulevard North
Jacksonville, Florida 32211
(904)744-9022
htp://www.nats.org/

National Dance Association
1900 Association Drive
Reston, Virginia 22091
(703)476-3436
http://www.aahperd.org/nda/nda.html

Society for Ethnomusicology
Morrison Hall 005
Indiana University
Bloomington, Indiana 47405-2501
http://www.indiana.edu/~ethmusic/

Speech Communication Association
5105 Backlick Road, Building F
Annandale, Virginia 22003
(703)750-0533
http://www.scassn.org/

Counseling & Human Services

American Art Therapy Association
1202 Allanson Road
Mundelein, Illinois 60060
(847)949-6064
http://www.louisville.edu/groups/aata-www/

American Association for Marriage and Family Therapy
1133 15th Street NW, Suite 300
Washington, D.C. 20005
(202)452-0109
http://www.aamft.org/

American Association for Music Therapy, Inc.
One Station Plaza
Ossinning, New York 10563
(914)944-9260

American College Counseling Association
5999 Stevenson Avenue
Alexandria, Virginia 22304-3300
(703)823-9800
http:///www.raritanval.edu/internet/acca/

American College Personnel Association
One Dupont Circle, Suite 300
Washington, D.C. 20036
(202)835-2272
http://www.acpa.nche.edu/

American Counseling Association
5999 Stevenson Avenue
Alexandria, Virginia 22304-3300
(703)823-9800
http://www.counseling.org/

American Dance Therapy Association
10632 Little Patuxent Parkway
Columbia, Maryland 21044
(410)997-4040
http://www.citi.net/ADTA/

American Mental Health Counselors Association
5999 Stevenson Avenue
Alexandria, Virginia 22304
(703)823-9800

American Occupational Therapy Association
4720 Montgomery Lane
Bethesda, Maryland 20814-3425
(301)652-2682
http://www.aota.org/

American Physical Therapy Association
1111 N. Fairfax Street
Alexandria, Virginia 22314
(703)684-2782
http://apta.edoc.com/

American Psychological Association
750 First Street NE
Washington, D.C. 20002
(202)336-5500
http://www.apa.org/

American Rehabilitation Counseling Association
5999 Stevenson Avenue
Alexandria, Virginia 22304-3300
(703)823-9800

Association for Adult Development and Aging
     5999 Stevenson Avenue
     Alexandria, Virginia 22304
     (703)823-9800

Association for Counselor Education and Supervision
     5999 Stevenson Avenue
     Alexandria, Virginia 22304-3300
     (703)823-9800

Association for Multicultural Counseling and Development
     5999 Stevenson Avenue
     Alexandria, Virginia 22304
     (703)823-9800
     http://edap.bgsu.edu/AMCD/

National Association for Music Therapy
     8455 Colesville Road, Suite 930
     Silver Spring, Maryland 20910-3319
     (301)589-3300
     http://www.cais.com/namt/index.html

National Association of Social Workers
     750 First Street NE, Suite 700
     Washington, D.C. 20002-4241
     (202)408-8600
     http://www.naswdc.org/

National Council on Rehabilitation Education
     Department of Special Education and Rehabilitation
     Utah State University
     Logan, Utah 84322-2870
     (801)797-3241
     http://www.nchrtm.okstate.edu/NCRE/board.HTM

Education & Student Services

American Association for Adult and Continuing Education
     1200 18th Street, N.W., Suite 300
     Washington, D.C. 20036-2422
     (202)429-5131
     http://www.ncl.org/anr/partners/aaace.htm

American Association for Higher Education
> One Dupont Circle NW, Suite 360
> Washington, D.C. 20036
> (202)293-6440
> http://www.aahe.org/

American Association of Colleges for Teacher Education
> One Dupont Circle NW, Suite 610
> Washington, D.C. 20036-1186
> (202)293-293-2450
> http://www.aacte.org/

American Association of Collegiate Registrars and Admissions Officers
> One Dupont Circle NW, Suite 330
> Washington, D.C. 20036
> (202)292-293-9161
> http://www.whes.org/members/aacrao.html

American Association of University Professors
> 1012 14th Street NW, Suite 500
> Washington, D.C. 20005
> (202)737-5900
> http://www.igc.apc.org/aaup

American College Counseling Association
> 5999 Stevenson Avenue
> Alexandria, Virginia 22304
> http://www.raritanval.edu/internet/acca/

American College Personnel Association
> One Dupont Circle, Suite 360A
> Washington, D.C. 20036-1110
> (202)835-2272
> http://www.acpa.nche.edu/

American Counseling Association
> 5999 Stevenson Avenue
> Alexandria, Virginia 22304-3300
> http://www.counseling.org/

American Educational Research Association
1230 17th Street NW
Washington, D.C. 20036-3078
(202)223-9485
http://aera.net

American Psychological Association
750 First Street NE
Washington, D.C. 20002
(202)336-5500
http://www.apa.org/

American Society for Engineering Education
1818 N Street N.W., Suite 600
Washington, D.C. 20036-2479
(202) 331-3500
http://www.asee.org/

American Society for Training and Development
1640 King Street
Box 1443
Alexandria, Virginia 22313-3043
(703)683-8100
http://www.astd.org/

Association for Childhood Education International
17904 Georgia Avenue, Suite 215
Olney, Maryland 20832
(800)423-3563
http://www.udel.edu/bateman/acei/

Association for Continuing Higher Education
Trident Technical College
P.O. Box 118067, CE-M
Charleston, South Carolina 29423-8067
(803)574-6658
http://www.charleston.net/org/ache/

Association for Counselor Education and Supervision
5999 Stevenson Avenue
Alexandria, Virginia 22304-3300
(703)823-9800

Association for Supervision and Curriculum Development
1250 N. Pitt Street
Alexandria, Virginia 22314-1405
(703)549-9110
http://www.ascd.org/

Association of Teacher Educators
1900 Association Drive, Suite ATE
Reston, Virginia 22091-1502
(703)620-3110
http://www.siu.edu/departments/coe/ate/index/html

Council for Exceptional Children
1920 Association Drive
Reston, Virginia 20191-1589
(703)620-3660
http://www.cec.sped.org/

International Reading Association
800 Barksdale Road
P.O. Box 8139
Newark, Delaware 19714-8139
(302)731-1600
http://www.reading.org/

NAFSA: Association of International Educators
1875 Connecticut Avenue NW, Suite 1000
Washington, D.C. 20009-5728
(202)462-4811
http://www.nafsa.org/

National Academic Advising Association
Kansas State University
2323 Anderson Avenue, Suite 225
Manhattan, Kansas 66502-2912
(913)532-5717
http://www.ksu.edu/nacada/

National Association for Bilingual Education
1220 L Street NW, Suite 605
Washington, D.C. 20005
(202)898-1829
http://www.nabe.org/

National Association for Physical Education in Higher Education
c/o Department of Human Performance
San Jose State University
San Jose, California 95192-0054
(408)924-3029
http://www.napehe.org/

National Association for Women in Education
1325 18th Street NW, Suite 210
Washington, D.C. 20036-6511
(202)659-9330

National Association of Student Personnel Administrators
1875 Connecticut Avenue, Suite 418
Washington, D.C. 20009
(202)265-7500
http://www.naspa.org/

National Council of Teachers of Mathematics
1906 Association Drive
Reston, Virginia 20191-1593
(703)620-9840
http://www.nctm.org/

National Council for the Social Studies
3501 Newark Street NW
Washington, D.C. 20016
(202)966-7840
http://www.ncss.org/online/

National Council on Measurement in Education
1230 17th Street NW
Washington, D.C. 20036-3078
(202)223-9318

National Reading Conference
200 North Michigan
Suite 300
Chicago, IL 60601
(312) 41-1272
http://www.iusb.edu/~edud/EleEd/nrc/nrcindex.html

National Science Teachers Association
1840 Wilson Boulevard
Arlington, Virginia 22201-3000
(703)243-7100
http://www.nsta.org/

Society for History Education
History Teacher, California State University
1250 Bellflower Boulevard
Long Beach, California 90840-1601
(562)985-1653
http://www.csulb.edu/~agunns/relprm/tht01.html

Society for Nutrition Education
2001 Killebrew Drive, Suite 340
Minneapolis, Minnesota 55425-1882
(612)854-0035
http://www.social.com/health/nhic/data/hr0500/hr0554.html/

Society for Public Health Education
2001 Addison Street, Suite 220
Berkeley, California 94704
(510)644-9242
http://www.social.com/health/nhic/data/hr0400/hr0420.html

Health & Recreation

American Alliance for Health, Physical Education, Recreation and Dance
1900 Association Drive
Reston, Virginia 20191
(703)476-3400
http://www.aahperd.org/

American Association for Leisure and Recreation
1900 Association Drive
Reston, Virginia 20191
(703)476-3400
http://www.aahperd.org/aalr/aalr.html

American Athletic Trainers Association and Certification Board
660 W Duarte Road
Arcadia, California 91007
(818)445-1978

American Dietetic Association
216 W. Jackson Boulevard
Chicago, Illinois 60606-6995
(312)899-0040
http://www.eatright.org/

American Nurses Association
600 Maryland Avenue SW
Washington, D.C. 20024
(202)651-7060
http://www.nursingworld.org/

American Public Health Association
1015 15th Street NW
Washington, D.C. 20005-2605
(202)789-5600
http://www.apha.org/

American Speech-Language Hearing Association
10801 Rockville Pike
Rockville, Maryland 20852
(301)897-5700
http://www.asha.org/

Association for the Advancement of Health Education
1900 Association Drive
Reston, Virginia 20191
(702)476-3400
http://www.aahperd.org/aahe/aahe.html

Association of Schools of Allied Health Professions
1730 M Street, Suite 500
Washington, D.C. 20036
(202)293-4848
http://proteus.mig.missouri.edu/shrp/asahp/

Council on Social Work Education
1600 Duke Street, Suite 300
Alexandria, Virginia 22314
(703)683-8080
http://www.cswe.org/

National Association for Sport and Physical Education
1900 Association Drive
Reston, Virginia 20191
(703)476-3410
http://www.aahperd.org/naspe/naspe.html

National Association of Advisors for the Health Professions
P.O. Box 1518
Champaign, Illinois 61824-1518
(217)355-0063
http://wwwcareers.com/A/0130.html

The National Athletic Trainers Association
2952 Stemmons Freeway
Dallas, Texas 75247
(214) 637-6282
http://www.nata.org/

National League for Nursing
350 Hudson Street
New York, New York 10014
(212)989-9393
http://www.nln.org/

Society for Nutrition Education
2001 Killebrew Drive, Suite 340
Minneapolis, Minnesota 55425-1882
(612)854-0035
http://www.social.com/health/nhic/data/hr0500/hr0554.html/

Society for Public Health Education
2001 Addison Street, Suite 220
Berkeley, California 94704
(510)644-9242
http://www.social.com/health/nhic/data/hr0400/hr0420.html

History, Ethnic and Cultural Studies

African Studies Association
Credit Union Building
Emory University
Atlanta, Georgia 30322
(404)329-6410
http://www.acls.org/afrstuda.htm

American Association for State and Local History
530 Church Street, Suite 600
Nashville, Tennessee 37219-2325
(615)255-2971
http://www.nashville.net/~aaslh/

American Historical Association
400 A Street SE
Washington, D.C. 20003-3889
(202)544-2422
http://chnm.gmu.edu/chnm/aha/

American Oriental Society
Hatcher Graduate Library
University of Michigan
Ann Arbor, Michigan 48109-1205
(313)747-4760

American Society for Ethnohistory
The Newberry Library
60 West Walton Street
Chicago, Illinois 60610-3305
(219)875-7237

American Studies Association
1120 19th Street N.W.,Suite 301
Washington, D.C. 20036
(202)467-4783
http://www.georgetown.edu/crossroads/asainfo.html

Association for Asian Studies
1 Lane Hall
University of Michigan
Ann Arbor, Michigan 48109
(313)665-2490
http://www.easc.indiana.edu/~aas/

Association for Canadian Studies in the United States
1317 F Street N.W., Suite 920
Washington, D.C. 20004-1105
(202)393-2580
http://wwww.iccs-ciec.ca/info/assoc/e-usa.html

Association for Jewish Studies
Mailstop MB0001
Brandeis University
P.O. Box 9110
Waltham, Massachusetts 02554-9110
(617)736-2981

Association for the Study of Afro-American Life and History
1407 14th Street NW
Washington, D.C. 20005
(202)667-2822
http://www.artnoir.com/asalh.html

Community Colleges Humanities Association
Community College of Philadelphia
1700 Spring Garden Street, Room MR-5
Philadelphia, Pennsylvania 19130
(215)751-8860

Economic History Association
Department of Economics
213 Summerfield Hall
University of Kansas
Lawrence, Kansas 66045
(913)864-3501
http://cs.muohio.edu/EHA/

International Studies Association
324 Social Sciences Building
University of Arizona
Tucson, Arizona 85721
(520)621-7715
http://csf.Colorado.EDU/isa/

Latin American Studies Association
946 William Pitt Union
University of Pittsburgh
Pittsburgh, Pennsylvania 15260
(412)648-7929
http://www.pitt.edu/~lasa/

Middle East Studies Association of North America
1643 East Helen Street
University of Arizona
Tucson, Arizona 85721
(520)621-5850
http://www.mesa.arizona.edu/

National Council for Black Studies
California State University, Dominguez Hills
Carson, California 90747
http://www.eiu.edu/~ncbs

Organization of American Historians
112 Bryan Street
Bloomington, Indiana 47408
(812)855-7311
http://www.indiana.edu/~oah/

Society for the Advancement of Scandinavian Study
Brigham Young University
Box 26118
Provo, Utah 84602-6118
http://www.buy.edu/sasslink/

Languages, Literature & Writing

American Association for Applied Linguistics
7630 West 145th Street, Suite 202
Apple Valley, Minnesota 55124
(612)953-0805
http://jan.ucc.nau.edu/~aaal97/

American Association of Teachers of Arabic
c/o Brigham Young University
280 HRCB
Provo, Utah 84602
(801)378-6531
http://humanities.byu.edu/aata/aata_homepage.html

American Association of Teachers of French
57 E. Armory Avenue
Champaign, Illinois 61820
(217)333-2842
http://www.utsa.edu/aatf/aatf_fr.html

American Association of Teachers of German
112 Haddontowne Court, No.104
Cherry Hill, New Jersey 08034
(609)795-9398
http://www.aatg.org/

American Association of Teachers of Italian
Brock University
St. Catherines, Ontario
Canada L3C 4X8
(416)732-2149

American Association of Teachers of Slavic and East European Languages
Auburn University
6030 Haley Center
Auburn, Alabama 36849-5204
http://clover.slavic.pitt.edu/~aatseel/

American Association of Teachers of Spanish and Portuguese

Butler-Hancock, Room 210
University of Northern Colorado
Greeley, Colorado 80639
(970)351-1090
http://www.aatsp.org/

American Classical League

Miami University of Ohio
Oxford, Ohio 45056
http://www.umich.edu/~acleague/

American Comparative Literature Association

5242 University of Oregon
Eugene, Oregon 97403-5242
(541)346-0737
http://www.acla.org/

American Council of Teachers of Russian

1776 Massachusetts Avenue NW, Suite 700
Washington, D.C. 20036
(202)833-7522
http://www.actr.org/

American Philological Association

Department of Classics
College of the Holy Cross
Worcester, Massachusetts 01610-2395
(508)793-2203
http://scholar.cc.emory.edu/scripts/APA/APA-MENU.html

American Translators Association

1800 Diagonal Road, Suite 220
Alexandria, Virginia 223314-2840
(703)683-6100
http://www.atanet.org/

Associated Writing Programs

George Mason University
Tallwood House, Mail Stop 1E3
Fairfax, Virginia 22031
(703)993-4301
http://www.gmu.edu/departments/awp/

Association of Teachers of Japanese
Department of East Asian Languages and Literature
Campus Box 279
University of Colorado
Boulder, Colorado 80309-0279
(303)492-1138

Chinese Language Teachers Association
c/o Kalamazoo College
1200 Academy Street
Kalamazoo, Michigan 49006
(616)337-7325
http://www.cohams.ohio-state.edu/clta

Community Colleges Humanities Association
Community College of Philadelphia
1700 Spring Garden Street
Philadelphia, Pennsylvania 19130
(215)751-8860

Conference on College Composition and Communication
1111 W. Kenyon Road
Urbana, Illinois 61801
(217)328-3870
http://www.ncte.org/groups/cccc.html

Linguistic Society of America
1325 18th Street NW, Suite 211
Washington, D.C. 20036-6501
FAX: (202)835-1717
http://www.lsadc.org/

Modern Language Association of America
10 Astor Place
New York, New York 10003-6981
(212)475-9500

National Council of Teachers of English
1111 W. Kenyon Road
Urbana, Illinois 61801
(217)328-3870
http://www.ncte.org/

Teachers of English to Speakers of Other Languages
  1600 Cameron Street, Suite 300
  Alexandria, Virginia 22314-2715
  (703)836-0774
  http://www.edweek.org/context/orgs/tesoli.htm

Libraries and Museums

African-American Museums Association
  P.O. Box 548
  Wilberforce, Ohio 45384-0548
  (513)376-4611
  http://www.artnoir.com/aama.html

American Association of Law Libraries
  53 West Jackson,Suite 940
  Chicago, Illinois 60604
  (312)939-4764
  http://www.aalnet.org/

American Association of Museums
  1225 I Street NW, Suite 400
  Washington, D.C. 20005
  (202)289-9132
  http://www.aam-us.org/

American Institute for Conservation of Historic and Artistic Works
  1717 K Street N.W.,Suite 301
  Washington, D.C. 20006
  (202)452-9545
  http://palimpsest.stanford.edu/aic/

American Library Association
  50 East Huron Street
  Chicago, Illinois 60611-2795
  (800)545-2433
  http://www.ala.org/

American Society for Information Science
  8720 Georgia Avenue, Suite 501
  Silver Spring, Maryland 20910
  (301)495-0900
  http://www.asis.org/

American Theological Library Association
    820 Church Street, Suite 400
    Evanston, Illinois 60201-5613
    (847)869-7788
    http://www.library.vanderbilt.edu/atla/home.html

Art Libraries Society/North America
    4101 Lake Boone Trail, Suite 201
    Raleigh, North Carolina 27607
    (919)787-5181
    http://www.uflib.ufl.edu/arlis/

Association of College and Research Libraries
    50 East Huron Street
    Chicago, Illinois 60611-2795
    (800)545-2433
    http://wwww.ala.org/acrl.html

Music Library Association
    P.O. Box 487
    Canton, Massachusetts 02021
    (617)828-8450
    http://www.music.indiana.edu/tech_s.mla.index.htm

Society of American Archivists
    600 S. Federal Street, Suite 504
    Chicago, Illinois 60605
    (312)922-0140
    http://www.archivists.org/

Special Libraries Association
    1700 18th Street NW
    Washington, D.C. 20009
    (202)234-4700
    http://www.sla.org/

Mathematics, Technology & Business

AACSB—The International Association for Management Education
600 Emerson Road, Suite 300
St. Louis, Missouri 63141-6762
(314)872-8481
http://www.aacsb.edu/

American Association for Artificial Intelligence
445 Burgess Drive
Menlo Park, California 94025-3442
(415)328-4457
http://www.aaai.org/

American Economic Association
2014 Broadway, Suite 305
Nashville, Tennessee 37203-2418
(615)322-2595

American Mathematical Society
P.O. Box 6248
Providence, Rhode Island 02940-6248
(401)455-4000
http://www.ams.org/

American Society for Engineering Education
1818 N Street N.W., Suite 600
Washington, D.C. 20036-2479
(202)331-3500
http://www.asee.org/

American Society for Information Science
8720 Georgia Avenue, Suite 501
Silver Spring, Maryland 20910-3602
(301)495-0900
http://www.asis.org/

American Statistical Association
1429 Duke Street
Alexandria, Virginia 22314-3402
(703)684-1221
http://www.amstat.org/

American Vocational Association
    1410 King Street
    Alexandria, Virginia 22314
    (800)826-9972
    http://www.avaonline.org/

Association for Computational Linguistics
    P.O. Box 6090
    Somerset, New Jersey 08875
    (908)873-3898
    http://www.cs.columbia.edu/~radev.newacl/

Mathematical Association of America
    1529 18th Street NW
    Washington, D.C. 20036-1385
    (800)331-1622
    http://www.maa.org/

National Business Education Association
    1914 Association Drive
    Reston, Virginia 20191
    (703)860-8300
    http://www.nbea.org/

National Council of Teachers of Mathematics
    1906 Association Drive
    Reston, Virginia 20191-1593
    (703)620-9840
    http://www.nctm.org/

Philosophy & Religion

American Academy of Religion
    1703 Clifton Road NE
    Suite G-5
    Atlanta, Georgia 30329-4019
    (404)727-7920
    http://www.aar-site.org/

American Philosophical Association
University of Delaware
Newark, Delaware 19716
(302)831-1112
http://www.udel.edu/apa/

American Philosophical Society
104 South Fifth Street
Philadelphia, Pennsylvania 19106-3387
(215)440-3400
http://www.amphilsoc.org/

Society of Biblical Literature
1201 Clairmont Road, Suite 300
Decatur, Georgia 30030
(404)636-4744
http://shemesh.scholar.emory.edu/scripts/SBL/SBL-MENU.html

Sciences

American Association for Clinical Chemistry
2101 L Street NW, Suite 202
Washington, D.C. 20037-1526
(202)857-0717
http://www.aacc.org/

American Association for the Advancement of Science
1200 NewYork Avenue N.W.
Washington, D.C. 20005
(202)326-6400
http://www.aaas.org/

American Association of Anatomists
9650 Rockville Pike
Bethesda, Maryland 20814-3998
(301)571-8314
http://www.anatomy.org/anatomy/

American Association of Physics Teachers
One Physics Ellipse
College Park, Maryland 20740-3845
(301)209-3300
http://www.aapt.org/

American Astronomical Society
2000 Florida Avenue N.W., Suite 400
Washington, D.C. 20009
(202)328-2010
http://www.aas.org/

American Chemical Society
1155 16th Street NW
Washington, D.C. 20036
(202)872-4600
http://www.acs.org/

American Geological Institute
4220 King Street
Alexandria, Virginia 22302-1502
(703)379-2480
http://jei.umd.edu/

American Institute of Biological Sciences
107 Carpenter Drive, Suite 100
Sterling, Virginia 20164
(703)834-0812
http://www.aibs.org/

American Institute of Physics
One Physics Ellipse
College Park, Maryland 20740-3843
(301)209-3100
http://www.aip.org/

American Physical Society
One Physics Ellipse
College Park, Maryland 20740-3844
(301)209-3200
http://www.aps.org/

American Physiological Society
9650 Rockville Pike
Bethesda, Maryland 20814-3991
(301)530-7164
http://www.ascb.org/aps/

American Society for Biochemistry and Molecular Biology
9650 Rockville Pike
Bethesda, Maryland 20814-3996
(301)530-7145
http://www.ascb.org/asbmb

American Society for Cell Biology
9650 Rockville Pike
Bethesda, Maryland 20814-3992
(301)530-7153
http://www.ascb.org/

American Society for Horticultural Science
600 Cameron Street
Alexandria, Virginia 22314
(703)836-4606
http://www.ashs.org/

American Society for Microbiology
1325 Massachusetts Avenue NW
Washington, D.C. 20005
(202)942-9283
http://www.asmusa.org/

Botanical Society of America
Business Office
1735 Neil Avenue
Columbus, Ohio 43210-1293
FAX:(614)292-3519
http://www.botany.org/

Ecological Society of America
2010 Massachusetts Avenue, N.W., Suite 400
Washington, D.C. 20036
(202)833-8773
http://esa.sdsc.edu/ESA.html

Entomological Society of America
9301 Annapolis Road
Lanham, Maryland 20706-3115
FAX: (301)731-4538
http://www.entsoc.org/

Geological Society of America
    3300 Penrose Place
    Boulder, Colorado 80301
    (303)447-2020
    http://www.geosociety.org/

National Science Teachers Association
    1840 Wilson Boulevard
    Arlington, Virginia 22201-3000
    (703)243-7100
    http://www.asta.org/

Social Sciences

Academy of Political Science
    475 Riverside Drive, Suite 1274
    New York, New York 10115-0012
    http://epn.org/psq/psaops.html

American Anthropological Association
    4350 North Fairfax Drive
    Arlington, Virginia 22203-1620
    (703)528-1902
    http://www.ameranthassn.org/

American Geographical Society
    120 Wall Street
    New York, New York 10005
    (212)422-5456

American Political Science Association
    1527 New Hampshire Avenue NW
    Washington, D.C. 20036
    (202)483-2512
    http://www.apsanet.org/

American Sociological Association
    1722 N Street NW
    Washington, D.C. 20036-2981
    (202)833-3410
    http://www.asanet.org/

Archaeological Institute of America
Boston University
656 Beacon Street
Boston, Massachusetts 02215-2010
(617)353-9361
http://csaws.brynmawr.edu:443/aia.html

Association of American Geographers
1710 16th Street NW
Washington, D.C. 20009-3198
(202)234-1450
http://www.aag.org/

Appendix II
Selected Resources

Periodicals

The Chronicle of Higher Education. Washington, D.C.: The Chronicle of Higher
    Education, Inc.
    http://www.chronicle.com

Community College Times. Washington, D.C.: American Association of
    Community Colleges
    http://www.aacc.nche.edu/commun/commun/htm#t

Community College Week. Fairfax, Virginia: Cox, Matthews & Associates, Inc.
    http://www.ccweek.com/

Lingua Franca. New York, New York: Lingua Franca,Inc.
    http://www.linguafranca.com

Directories

Barron's Profiles of American Colleges. Hauppauge, New York: Barron's
    Educational Series, Inc.

The College Handbook. New York, New York: College Entrance Examination
    Board.

Directory of Canadian Universities = Répertoire des universités canadiennes. Ottawa, Ontario, Canada: Association of Universities and Colleges of Canada.

Guide to Community, Technical and Junior Colleges. Washington, D.C.: American Association of Community and Junior Colleges

Higher Education Directory. Falls Church, Virginia: Higher Education Publications, Inc.
http://www.hepinc.com/

Peterson's Guide to Four-Year Colleges. Princeton, New Jersey: Peterson's Guides, Inc.
http://www.petersons.com/

Peterson's Guide to Graduate Study (6 volumes). Princeton, New Jersey: Peterson's Guides, Inc.
http://www.petersons.com/

Peterson's Guide to Two-year Colleges. Princeton, New Jersey: Peterson's Guides, Inc.
http://www.petersons.com/

World List of Universities. London, England: MacMillan Press, Ltd.

The World of Learning. London, England: Europa Publications, Ltd.
http://eco.web.com/register/02350.html

Index